Leadership Development SIMPLIFIED

Leadership Development SIMPLIFIED

5 Easy-to-Learn Mindsets for Leadership by Everyone, Everywhere

PAT O'CONNELL, PhD

Lourdes University

2030 Leadership
Woodforest Publishing
Sylvania, Ohio

Leadership Development SIMPLIFIED

5 Easy-to-Learn Mindsets for Leadership by Everyone, Everywhere

Copyright ©2024 by Patricia K. O'Connell, Ph.D.

All rights reserved. No part of this book may be reproduced or utilized in any form or by any manner whatsoever, electronic or mechanical, including photocopying, recording, or by any information storage and retrieval system, without permission in writing from the author.

Names: O'Connell, Pat, author/Calkins, Heather, editor

Title: Leadership development simplified: 5 easy-to-learn mindsets for leadership by everyone, everywhere/Patricia K. O'Connell, Lourdes University

Description: 1 Edition/Sylvania, Ohio: Woodforest Publishing, 2024/Includes bibliographical references

Identifiers: ISBN: 979-8-9908918-3-8 (paperback edition), ISBN: 979-8-9908918-2-1 (e-book)

Subjects: LCSH: Leadership--Development | Psychological Aspects | Self-Esteem | Self-Management | Developmental Psychology | BISAC: Business & Economics/Leadership | Education/Leadership Professional Development | Psychology/Developmental/General | Self-Help/Personal Growth/Success

ISBN: 979-8-9908918-3-8 (paperback edition)

ISBN: 979-8-9908918-2-1 (e-book)

Published and Printed in the United States
by Woodforest Publishing
This book is printed on acid-free paper.

Dedication

> *To all who learn and use the simple Leader Development Webs of Belief:*
> *Please use your leadership skills and influence to bring simplicity and harmony to our world.*

Acknowledgements

As I publish this long-awaited book, I thank my colleagues and students who have supported and applauded my work for a quarter of a century. Thanks also to my children, Katrina and Bryan, who have always supported my career and scholarship, and Jay, who insisted I write this book. Kudos to my grandsons Brandon and Joe, who learned and passed on the story of the webs of belief. Special acknowledgements to my leadership students who assisted in this research and are cited in the Endnotes. This book would never have been finished without Heather Calkins, M.O.L., one of my former graduate students who first learned about the webs of belief in my classroom. Her editing skills and scholarly knowledge of leadership make this guide readable and understandable.

About the Author

Dr. Pat O'Connell has practiced and studied leadership for over four decades. She holds a B.S. in Business from Miami University, an MBA in Marketing from University of Toledo, and a Ph.D. in Developmental Psychology and Human Resources Development from the University of Toledo. Her business expertise includes corporate leadership positions in market research, executive leadership, consulting, personnel policies development, organizational behavior, meeting facilitation, strategic planning, team leadership, team formation, team re-building, and organizational development. She has served as a corporate vice president and founded her own management consulting firm. As Professor of Leadership, her scholarly research and publishing have continued for over two decades. She is a regular presenter and keynote speaker in corporate venues and at international leadership conferences.

CONTENTS

	Dedication	v
	Acknowledgements	v
	About the Author	v
	How To Use This Book	1
1	Developing as a Leader in the 21ˢᵗ Century	3
2	The Competencies You Need & the Five Simple Webs of Belief	11
	What Leadership Competencies & Styles Do We Need Today?	*11*
	Introduction to the Webs of Belief for Leader Development	*13*
3	The Learning Web of Belief ˢᴹ	21
	What is Learning in the 21ˢᵗ Century	*21*
	The Learning Web of Belief ˢᴹ	*22*
	Understanding the Learning Web of Belief ˢᴹ	*22*
	Leader Competencies & Styles Within the Learning Web of Belief ˢᴹ	*28*
	How to Apply the Learning Web of Belief ˢᴹ in Your Leader Development	*29*
	The Learning Web of Belief ˢᴹ in Teams & Organizations	*32*
	The Learning Web of Belief ˢᴹ in Action	*33*
	Competencies & Mindsets Developed via the Learning Web of Belief ˢᴹ	*37*
4	The Reverence Web of Belief ˢᴹ	39
	What is Reverence in the 21ˢᵗ Century?	*39*
	The Reverence Web of Belief ˢᴹ	*40*
	Understanding the Reverence Web of Belief ˢᴹ	*41*
	Leader Competencies & Styles Within the Reverence Web of Belief ˢᴹ	*47*
	How to Apply the Reverence Web of Belief ˢᴹ in Your Leader Development	*49*
	The Reverence Web of Belief ˢᴹ in Teams & Organizations	*53*
	The Reverence Web of Belief ˢᴹ in Action	*54*
	Competencies & Mindsets Developed via the Reverence Web of Belief ˢᴹ	*59*

5	The Purpose Web of Belief^{SM}	61
	What is Purpose in the 21st Century	*61*
	The Purpose Web of Belief^{SM}	*62*
	Understanding the Purpose Web of Belief^{SM}	*63*
	Leader Competencies & Styles Within the Purpose Web of Belief^{SM}	*65*
	How to Apply the Purpose Web of Belief^{SM} in Your Leader Development	*66*
	The Purpose Web of Belief^{SM} in Teams & Organizations	*74*
	The Purpose Web of Belief^{SM} in Action	*74*
	Competencies & Mindsets Developed via The Purpose Web of Belief^{SM}	*79*
6	The Authenticity Web of Belief^{SM}	81
	What is Authenticity in the 21st Century	*81*
	The Authenticity Web of Belief^{SM}	*82*
	Understanding the Authenticity Web of Belief^{SM}	*83*
	Leader Competencies & Styles Within the Authenticity Web of Belief^{SM}	*86*
	How to Apply the Authenticity Web of Belief^{SM} in Your Leader Development	*88*
	The Authenticity Web of Belief^{SM} in Teams & Organizations	*93*
	The Authenticity Web of Belief^{SM} in Action	*95*
	Competencies & Mindsets Developed via the Authenticity Web of Belief^{SM}	*99*
7	The Flâneur Web of Belief^{SM}	101
	What is Flâneur in the 21st Century	*101*
	The Flâneur Web of Belief^{SM}	*102*
	Understanding the Flâneur Web of Belief^{SM}	*103*
	Leader Competencies & Styles Within the Flâneur Web of Belief^{SM}	*107*
	How to Apply the Flâneur Web of Belief^{SM} in Your Leader Development	*109*
	The Flâneur Web of Belief^{SM} in Teams & Organizations	*117*
	The Flâneur Web of Belief^{SM} in Action	*118*
	Competencies & Mindsets Developed via the Flâneur Web of Belief^{SM}	*123*
8	Mapping Your Leadership & Life Development	125
	The Power of Goal Setting	*125*
	Why You Need a Formal Plan	*125*
	How To Create Your Formal Plan	*126*
	How To Implement Your Formal Plan	*131*
NOTES		**137**

HOW TO USE THIS BOOK

Consider this book an active guide to developing as a leader. You will find sections of explanation and instruction with leadership cases and vignettes to illustrate real world applications. Self-assessment and reflection exercises help you apply each lesson to your life and career. As you fill in the blanks, realities and themes will resonate with you. These are your clues about your leader development needs. Use the chart below as a guide to learning each lesson, thinking about it, and putting it into action. In Chapter 8, you will compile data from your assessments and reflections into a life and leadership growth plan. *If you prefer not to write in this book, a workbook with just the chapter exercises is available in electronic or hard copy form at www.drpatoconnell.com.*

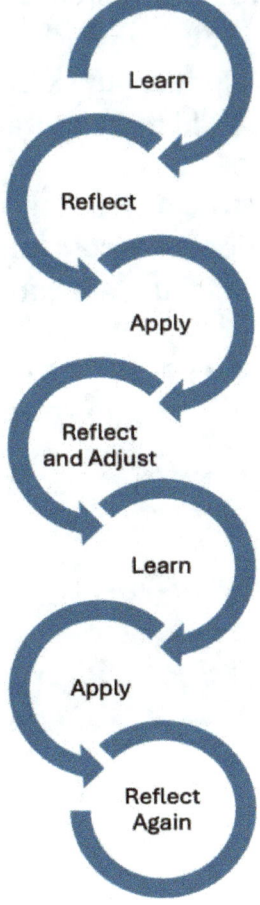

DEVELOPING AS A LEADER

is a lifelong sport . . .
a series of practices
during which
we test our skills
and build our endurance.

Participate joyfully.
Experience success humbly.
Face failure gracefully.

Find a pace and a path
unique to who you are.

PAT O'CONNELL

CHAPTER 1

DEVELOPING AS A LEADER IN THE 21ST CENTURY

A new order for a new millennium

Studies of history and society find periods of great upheaval, change, and invention during the decades surrounding a new century. From 1890 to 1910, industry revolutionized. We witnessed the advent of the assembly line, the hourly wage, unions, and women's right to vote. Inventions and innovations included the bicycle, car, airplane, telephone, and electric lighting. Cities expanded in area and population. In management, we discovered productivity in the workplace was keenly affected by supervisory practices and employee rewards.

The year 2000 marked a new century and a new millennium. The decades surrounding this time saw a technological and cultural transformation affecting every phase of work and life. The 21st century workspace is culturally diverse, technologically-explosive, and in a constant state of flux. The future is uncertain, and every entity is vulnerable to change. Organizations and their leaders face shifting competition and demands for innovation. Individuals and teams must continuously adapt to new realities in every sphere[1].

Leadership in the 21st century

An internet search for leadership yields over one million book titles and almost five million websites to explore[1]. The subject has been studied since the 1920's. Yet, after a century of investigation, social science scholars agree to disagree. *Leadership is a contested term with multiple meanings and diverse applications across people and contexts.* Debates continue: Are leadership and management separate processes? Are leaders born or developed? What is most important: traits, skills, or relationships? How do global influences and generational differences affect needs for leadership competencies? What leadership style best fits the situation and the people in it?

Across the world, management and leadership aim to get *tasks* done productively by forging *relationships* to motivate people. Today, the tasks, outputs, and performance of work, such as safety, quality, productivity, and customer satisfaction, are easily measured and tracked using computers or automation. The adoption of artificial intelligence will continue to measure task efficiency and improve productivity. Organizations without high standards for these task-related outcomes will not survive. Customers will not do business there. People will choose to work elsewhere. As we move forward, we will still need creativity and collaboration by individuals and teams. Today's employers know success depends on the human equation. They need capable leaders with multidimensional skills. They need people at all levels who are professional, adaptable, creative, critical thinkers, problem solvers, and team players. Leadership for the 21st century will focus on relationships, interpersonal communications, and employee development. Leaders must master the skills to educate and motivate their most precious resources: their people.

Are today's leaders born or made?

With all the challenges we face today, we need everyone's talents to propel our teams and our organizations to success. Today's leaders take on different roles and varied assignments. We work with diverse individuals and groups across organizations and cultures. It was once believed only great people possessed leadership traits. It is now clear leaders are made, not born. Every individual inherits personality traits and talents to use for their practice of leadership. Additional leadership skills and mindsets for the many situations we encounter can be taught and learned. Scholars and employers agree on one thing: every person in the workplace must understand and practice leadership[2]. Why? Because leadership behaviors and mindsets can be taught, understood, and modeled by anyone. Learning to lead is everyone's responsibility.

Three Paradigms for 21st Century Leader Development [3]

1. Learning to lead is parallel and intertwined with our development as adult human beings.
2. Our leadership is learned and practiced using our personal values and beliefs.
3. We continuously construct new skillsets and mindsets for leadership through observations and experiences in the world around us.

Learning to lead is linked to learning to live

Much is known about how children and adolescents grow and learn. We observe in amazement how young people develop in mind, body, and spirit. Although not as obvious and easy to observe, our human development continues through adulthood. As living organisms, we continuously change and evolve. We progress through life stages as we advance in age and experiences. Family, culture, education, career, community, affiliations, generation, and much more shape the development of our skillsets and mindsets. Our development as leaders is intertwined with our biological aging and our journey through adulthood[4].

Our leadership must incorporate connective beliefs

Trusted and respected leaders strive to build a peaceful world and improve our peoples' quality of life. To do this, we need to become global citizens who understand diverse perspectives, facilitate the creation of shared understanding, and serve collective needs. To solve complex challenges, address uncertainty, and transcend differences in cultures and identities, we must apply connective values and collaborative mindsets. For this guidebook and your developmental journey, we define leadership as: *Influencing self and others to adopt collaborative behaviors and mindsets to make meaningful connections, address mutual problems, and contribute to positive outcomes.*

We must use observation, experiences, and reflection

Formal education and training programs do not provide all the knowledge, skills, and dispositions we need for life and career. Schooling teaches us how to learn, not necessarily what to learn, as we move through adulthood. We become more effective leaders by observing and thinking about the situations and people around us. By reflecting on these experiences, we make new connections and find creative solutions to problems. The same practices may not work with different people or in different situations. We must adapt our interpretations, strategies, and responses to fit the dynamics we encounter. We act on our revised understandings. So, always look around. Seek fresh information and ideas. Think about what you see and hear. Use a leadership lens to compare and improve your own practices. Attend to information and gather capabilities relevant to your current needs for our life and work. Through trial and error, learn what to do when, where, and with whom.

Leader development in a complex world

Wise people embrace change.
JOSEPH SIFAKIS[5]

As 21st century professionals, we must constantly upgrade our technical skillsets to adapt to emerging technologies and developments in our fields. To practice leadership, we need a wide range of behaviors and mindsets to apply to the different situations we encounter. With today's deluge of resources and theories about what leadership is and the cascade of characteristics and competencies for effective leader practices, developing as a leader can be confusing and complicated. To improve your leadership skills, where do you start? How do you learn to lead in different contexts and situations? How do you adapt your skills to motivate people around you and contribute to your organization's success?

How to move forward as a leader for today and tomorrow

This book introduces five guiding principles which quickly convert theory to practice. Using *The Leader Development Webs of Belief*^{SM}, you continuously develop leadership competencies and styles to enrich your life and career. You better understand yourself and how to navigate your interaction with others. The *Leader Development Webs of Belief*^{SM} are derived from a massive research project excavating hundreds of characteristics and competencies from contemporary leadership theories and frameworks. Through research aggregation and synthesis, just five categories emerged. These groupings incorporate the full breadth and depth of skillsets and mindsets for effective leadership today. The webs of belief are *Learning, Reverence, Purpose, Authenticity,* and *Flâneur.* These guiding principles can be applied to management and leadership at any level and in any context. They support lifelong development for people of all backgrounds, beliefs, and identities. Individuals, teams, and organizations adopting the five webs of belief will become more productive, more successful, and more satisfied with their work and their lives. Learning to lead is for everyone, and it can be simple.

Leadership Case: 21st Century Markets: Volatile, Vulnerable, and Easily Changed by New Discoveries

For organizations to survive the uncertain conditions of today's global markets, they must plan strategically, to be solid and stable for the long term. At the same time, they must be flexible and nimble enough to change direction. Consider alternative energy in the middle decades of the 21st century. New technologies and sources are rapidly being developed, and improved. Solar and wind power, along with electric-powered vehicles, are taking hold. Mining lithium is now more profitable than mining coal. Alternative and synthetic materials are in use for everything from clothing to spacecraft. Long-time successful companies in almost every industry must adapt and change to these evolving resources, or they will not survive.

What vulnerabilities does your organization face in the next 10 years?

Leadership Case: The 21st Century & Unexpected Events: Conditions Can Change in a Day[6]

On December 14, 2012, a shooter broke into Sandy Hook elementary school in Newtown, Connecticut. 20 first graders' and six staff members' lives were lost. In the aftermath, U.S. President Barack Obama addressed the nation and Congress, calling for stricter gun laws in the U.S. Mayors and governors, school officials, and many business leaders supported a drastic reduction of gun sales. Federal legislation was introduced quickly, and the U.S. was abuzz with gun control fever. As the horror of the Sandy Hook shooting faded, and lobbies of pro-gun groups prevailed, no laws were changed. Gun manufacturers returned to business as usual.

Also consider the case of Stoneman Douglas High School in Parkland, Florida. On February 14, 2018, a shooter killed 17 people and injured 17 others. The student survivors became anti-violence activists and influenced the passage of new restrictions in Florida's gun laws. Although gun sales in the state have not decreased, attendance in safety classes has increased. In the 21st century, organizations of every kind must be ready to respond and adapt to uncertainty, volatility, and chaos. Imagine you were a top executive for gun manufacturers Remington or Smith & Wesson during these events. Even though unlikely, what if your markets and sales across the U.S. were greatly reduced within months? What strategic alternatives would you identify to save your company and industry? What plans would need to be put in motion right away?

Is your organization prepared to respond to a crisis in markets, supply chains, or government intervention?

SELF ASSESSMENT 1-1: YOUR 21ST CENTURY WORLD

Complete this assessment to describe the world you live and work in. Be brief. Simply note what first comes to mind.

MY WORK WORLD TODAY	MY PERSONAL WORLD TODAY
The environment: The People:	The environment: The People:
What is certain? What is uncertain? What is changing?	What is certain? What is uncertain? What is changing?
Current Challenges:	Current Challenges:

Leadership Case: Uncertain Career Tracks and No Guarantees

After earning her MBA, Kristin was hired by a Fortune 500 company. For ten years, Kristin received promotions and excelled within the company's marketing division. Her colleagues and managers expected her to be a top leader by mid-career. During this time, the firm's original product line and sales were challenged by international competitors, and its customer service and supply chain systems were outpaced by newer technologies. Kristin was now an industry expert and a seasoned, loyal employee. She had many ideas for overcoming these business challenges to become internationally competitive once more. Kristin began to apply for positions in executive management. With every attempt, she was told she had excellent qualifications, yet she was always second to an outside person with the same experience.

Kristin knew she was well-qualified for a broader role and used her extensive network to find a new opportunity at a smaller company. She was given much more responsibility. Within two years, the small company's owners decided to exit the industry, and the product lines Kristin knew best. They reduced the workforce and eliminated her role. Kristin again used her network to make contacts across the country and around the world. She was hired as a top marketing/sales executive for an international firm with a plan to expand their product lines. Kristin and her new management set a five-year plan for opening markets and developing customers.

> However, she knows her career will be marked by more uncertainty in our volatile world. She continues to build her strong network to be ready for the changes and challenges ahead.
> *How can you expand your network to be ready to explore different job or career opportunities when, and if, you need to?*

CONCLUSION

Research today shows we do not have to be born with leadership know-how. Through learning and reflection, we can become effective leaders. Our development as leaders is parallel with our development as adults. How we lead is driven by our personal and professional values and goals and shaped by our experiences in work and life. Today's leaders must incorporate an intricate and expansive set of competencies to be successful in our ever-changing world. Each of us needs to create a unique map for our personal and professional growth. Yet, in a world of chaos and complexity, it can be confusing, difficult, and overwhelming to know where to start. Leaders at all levels can use the simplified Leader Development Webs of Belief[SM] throughout their lifetime to build increasingly effective skills and mindsets.

A LEADER'S LENS

To lead is to resolve and decide.
To decide is to judge and to inspire.

But before we can resolve or decide
or judge or inspire,
we must look around and through
our leadership lens
at all the angles and perspectives
of our capabilities,
our possibilities, and our people.

To lead effectively
we need to step back and take time
To look through each lens
then reflect on our actions.
To be capable and patient enough
to pre-view and re-view our outcomes
from every strategic perspective
is to lead wisely and well.

PAT O'CONNELL

CHAPTER 2

THE COMPETENCIES YOU NEED & THE FIVE SIMPLE WEBS OF BELIEF

WHAT LEADERSHIP COMPETENCIES & STYLES DO WE NEED TODAY?

How do we capture the essence of what is required for leadership today? In its simplest form, leadership involves two parallel tracks: accomplishing tasks and relating with people. In the 20th century, we coupled autocratic leadership, or giving directions, with focusing on people's technical skillsets and task performance. Tasks and relationships are still at the heart of leadership. Yet, leading diverse individuals and teams to high performance is more complex and challenging than ever before. From 100 years of scholarly study, a multitude of concepts, frameworks, definitions, and schemas for leadership emerged. Dozens of leadership theories and styles comprising thousands of competencies are defined for use in managing and leading people, projects, and organizations. Creating a definitive list of leadership attributes is an exhaustive exercise.

So, how can an individual leader determine what to learn and what to apply in their own life and work? Where does one start to develop as a leader? Which style(s) will work for you? Is there a way to learn as many skills as possible, as quickly as possible? To simplify leader development, a listing of hundreds of mindsets and skillsets was drawn from scholarly studies and given simple, understandable labels. These five constructs, the *Leader Development Webs of Belief*[SM], are basic mental maps to use as guiding principles for personal and professional development through your life and career.

The Leader Development Webs of Belief[SM] were drawn from an initial group of emerging 21st century leadership theories: complexity, adaptive, and strategic leadership theories; relational, shared, and distributed theories; and authentic leadership theories. The research also incorporated adult development and identity development. Additional leadership theories are now included in the framework, with skills added for change leadership, connective leadership, crisis leadership, emotional intelligence, servant leadership, and transformational leadership. The five simple webs of belief for developing a comprehensive set of leadership skills are *Learning, Reverence, Purpose, Authenticity* and *Flâneur*[1]. The webs of belief foster advanced skills to adapt to ever-changing situations in career and life.

WHAT IS A WEB OF BELIEF?

A web of belief is a mindset for learning and development expressed in a simple, concrete statement. Each construct has a central organizing principle which is easy to understand and learn. A web of belief becomes a mental map to translate into more complex concepts, perspectives, and schemas. The basic concept remains the same, but the meaning, and the integration of the valued behavior, expands and evolves through the career and the lifespan. Using webs of belief for leadership development is efficient and smart. A leader can begin from where they are and progress at their own pace. Leaders advance their mindsets and skillsets in their own space and time as they discover new ways to interpret and apply each web of belief[2].

HOW CAN WE USE WEBS OF BELIEF TO DEVELOP AS LEADERS?

Adopting a web of belief is a strong commitment to learn and understand a broad set of knowledge, skills, and dispositions. Leaders use the webs of belief framework to assess where they are in their leadership journey, then identify next-level needs. They add new information to what they already know, then re-frame their understanding and perspectives. They become motivated to add or delete behaviors and mindsets. They engage in transformational learning and continuously construct new competencies. The framework encourages growth and development yet allows a leader to always review and refine prior learning within the web. This path to leader development is spiral and circular. As new capabilities emerge, the ability and motivation to develop expands and leaders gain increasingly advanced capacities across situations and contexts[3].

SELF-ASSESSMENT 2-1: YOUR DEVELOPMENTAL JOURNEY

Create a profile of yourself as a developing adult today.

My Age	My generation
A world or news event when I was 12 years old	My life stage
My career stage	My technology expertise
My profession or skillset	My hero(es)
My mentors or teachers	My best friend(s)
My leisure activities	Groups I belong to
Two of my values	Two things I believe in

INTRODUCTION TO THE WEBS OF BELIEF FOR LEADER DEVELOPMENT

The Learning Web of Belief ℠

> Belief in the capacity to gain knowledge, integrate it into practice, and continuously gain more advanced skills always and everywhere, throughout the career and life spans.

The Learning Web of Belief guides developing leaders to always extend our knowledge, skills, and dispositions. Learning is not just about memorizing new information. As a lifetime organizing principle, we use the Learning Web of Belief℠ to continuously understand our own identities, strengths, and weaknesses, then find opportunities to improve. We sharpen our skills for meta-cognition, self-awareness, self-regulation, and self-motivation. We observe and learn from our leaders, peers, and followers.

Our capacity for learning expands as we progress through life and career. We extend our understanding of ourselves, our relationships, and our interactions with others. We improve our communications skills. We become more sophisticated in moral reasoning and perspective-taking. We become more expansive, which means we know how to master new areas of expertise and more complex skills[4]. The more we learn, the more we want to learn and experience. The Learning Web of Belief is useful for change leadership, crisis leadership, transformational leadership, servant leadership, and authentic leadership. It develops our flexibility and creativity to respond to challenges and opportunities. *Chapter 3 will expand your understanding of The Learning Web of Belief, the leadership competencies developed by using it, and teach specifics for how to apply it in your life and leadership.*

REFLECTION EXERCISE 2-2: ABOUT THE LEARNING WEB OF BELIEF

1. How do I define learning in my life and work?

2. Who in my life or work is a role model for the practice of learning?

The Reverence Web of Belief SM

Belief in acceptance and incorporation of the needs of everyone, everywhere, with honor and awe of every person and all cultures' unique talents and contributions.

The Reverence Web of Belief is a developing leader's commitment to understand and celebrate inclusion. Leaders using the Reverence Web of Belief find common values for human interaction. Leaders practicing reverence share excitement about the unique identity of everyone we encounter in our workplaces and in our lives. Practicing reverence means acceptance of individuals and groups from different cultures and beliefs. Reverence also applies to the people in our personal lives and work. Sometimes practicing reverence is most difficult with those we are closest to!

Using reverence, leaders enjoy a sense of belonging to others and to the universe we share[5]. We are eager to learn about others' values, lifestyles, and backgrounds. Leaders with reverence become more collaborative, effectively manage conflict, think more broadly, and affirm others. We learn to see human diversities not as black and white, but with many shades of grey. We treat followers with honor and respect. We celebrate everyone's contributions. In turn, followers trust us and perform at high levels.

In the 21st century, leaders need to connect, collaborate, and align with others to gain influence and achieve results. The essence of the Reverence Web of Belief is wonder, awe, and honor for everyone everywhere. Using reverence, we adjust our leadership practices to listen to others' viewpoints and respond to others' needs. We respect new ideas and seek to understand information different from what we know or believe in. The Reverence Web of Belief helps leaders develop capacities needed for connective leadership, servant leadership, team leadership, and transformational leadership. It fosters social intelligence, cultural intelligence and global citizenship. *Chapter 4 will expand your understanding of the Reverence Web of Belief, the leadership competencies developed by using it, and teach specifics for how to apply it in your life and leadership.*

REFLECTIVE EXERCISE 2-3: ABOUT THE REVERENCE WEB OF BELIEF

1. How do I define reverence in my life and work?

2. Who in my life or work is a role model for the practice of reverence?

The Purpose Web of Belief ℠

Belief and engagement in personal mission, passion, and beneficial contributions to others in the form of roles, work, and service throughout the career and life spans.

The Purpose Web of Belief drives leaders to commit energy and effort to the work we do and the life we live. Leaders with purpose fully engage in tasks, projects, roles, and goals each day, each month, and each year. Leaders using the Purpose Web of Belief know the reasons for our behaviors. Living with purpose means having an aim for our actions throughout each day.

Leaders with purpose know our natural capabilities, our strengths, and our weaknesses. We use this understanding to answer our callings and follow our passions. We become intent about making contributions to our followers, organizations, and communities. A leader with purpose does not adhere to just one singular life's purpose. We evolve and grow, pursue new opportunities, and learn new skills. We may adjust our purpose from hour to hour each day, and over our life and career. The Purpose Web of Belief develops capacities for transformational leadership, authentic leadership, change leadership, adaptive leadership, and complexity leadership. Using purpose, leaders learn and practice self-regulation, visioning, strategic thinking, goal setting, action planning, and time management. *Chapter 5 will expand your understanding of the Purpose Web of Belief, the leadership competencies developed by using it, and specifics for how to apply it in your life and leadership.*

REFLECTIVE EXERCISE 2-4: ABOUT THE PURPOSE WEB OF BELIEF

1. How do I define purpose in my life and work?

2. Who in my life or work is a role model for the practice of purpose?

The Authenticity Web of Belief ^{SM}

> Belief in continuous discovery and understanding of one's identity and one's convictions, accompanied by clear expression and acknowledgement of the genuine self in interpersonal communications and behaviors.

In the 21st century, people of all ages and stages of life are drawn to leaders who say what they do and do what they say. Followers trust managers and peers who know who they are and act accordingly. The Authenticity Web of Belief guides developing leaders to continuously discover our unique identity. We project our true self to others with dignity and humility. We are genuine, transparent, and marked by our own leadership style. We build credibility with peers and followers by courageously communicating and behaving according to our convictions, values, and concept of ourselves[6].

We use the Authenticity Web of Belief to become experts in self-awareness. We build confidence in who we are and self-efficacy in what we can do. We learn to believe in ourselves. Authentic leaders use mindsets for hope, optimism, and resilience when faced with challenges and adversity. When working in teams, we build positivity, mutual respect, and collaboration. Authenticity is carefully developed over a career and lifetime. Skills gained using the Authenticity Web of Belief include reflective practice, balanced decision making, autonomy, effective communications, social intelligence, and strategic perspective taking. Developing authenticity increases capacities for self-leadership, connective leadership, and team leadership. Guided by the Authenticity Web of Belief, we become effective transformational leaders, change leaders, and servant leaders. *Chapter 6 will expand your understanding of the Authenticity Web of Belief, the leadership competencies developed by using it, and specifics on how to apply it in your life and leadership.*

REFLECTIVE EXERCISE 2-5: ABOUT THE AUTHENTICITY WEB OF BELIEF

1. How do I define authenticity in my life and work?

2. Who in my life or work is a role model for the practice of authenticity?

The Flâneur Web of Belief ^{SM}

> Belief in a philosophical, multi-perspective, and spirit-led approach to living and leading, balancing active participation with timely practice of observation, rest, reflection, and detachment.

The term flâneur (pronounced flah-nure') is drawn from French literature and means stroller, lounger, or one who saunters[7]. Leaders practicing flâneur remain calm in the face of the complexities and demands of life and work. We listen carefully to sort out issues and find answers in the situations we encounter. We take time for self-reflection. We make sense of our life stories and leadership experiences. We learn to balance our lives, manage our time, and set smart priorities. We use rest and contemplation to reduce stress and remain healthy. We become spiritual and philosophical as we navigate the twists and turns of career and life.

Leaders learning flâneur convert our intensity or frustration into detached observation, to become fascinated and curious about the challenges of our world. We are driven and purposeful, yet, at the same time, relaxed and distanced from the fury. We take time to see the big picture and imagine the possibilities. We calmly lead followers to consider all phases of an issue or problem. Subscribing to the Flâneur Web of Belief is a commitment to always think before we act. Slowing down may seem to take more time from our busy lives. It does not!

A measured approach to action increases the productivity, creativity, and quality of our efforts[8]. Using flâneur develops skills for change leadership, crisis leadership, complexity leadership, authentic leadership, and adaptive leadership. The ability to engage in active, yet thoughtful, dialogue improves competencies for servant leadership, connective leadership, shared leadership, and followership. Flâneur also builds social and emotional intelligence, active listening, interpersonal communication, optimism, and resilience. *Chapter 7 will expand your understanding of the Flâneur Web of Belief, the leadership competencies developed by using it, and teach specifics for how to apply it in your life and leadership.*

REFLECTIVE EXERCISE 2-6: ABOUT THE FLÂNEUR WEB OF BELIEF

1. How do I define flâneur in my life and work?

2. Who in my life or work is a role model for the practice of flâneur?

SELF ASSESSMENT 2-7: YOUR CONTRIBUTIONS TO LIFE AND WORK

Fill in this chart with your roles and your competencies in your work and life.

My Role(s) in:	Two competencies I bring to this role:	Two competencies I could develop for this role:
Work/Career	1. 2.	1. 2.
Life/ At Home	1. 2.	1. 2.
Community Service/Volunteer	1. 2.	1. 2.

CONCLUSION

Using the Leader Development Webs of Belief[SM], everyone can learn leadership. This framework is a distillation of the multitude of competencies from dozens of contemporary leadership theories and styles. The webs of belief are an efficient and unbounded set of guiding principles for novice, intermediate, and expert leaders. They foster self-analysis, reflection, and goal setting. This simple approach can be used for growth in any stage of career or life. It can become the central organizing framework to use for lifelong personal and professional development. As individuals apply the simple webs of belief, they acquire advanced and far-reaching leadership skills.

LEADERSHIP IS

a lifelong course in
learning
reverence
purpose
authenticity
and
flâneur.

PAT O'CONNELL

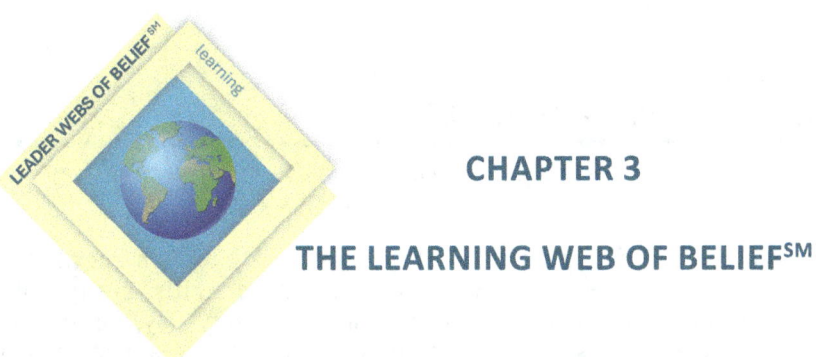

CHAPTER 3

THE LEARNING WEB OF BELIEF[SM]

> Belief in the capacity to gain knowledge, integrate it into practice, and continuously gain more advanced skills always and everywhere, throughout the career and life spans.

WHAT IS LEARNING IN THE 21ST CENTURY?

An automatic function of being
Learning is the brain's continuous addition of information to memory. We learn all the time, every day. Learning is the most natural function of the human body. Think about a baby's instinctive pursuit of learning: to eat, to smile, to grasp, to crawl, to walk, to understand language, and to interact with people. Throughout life, our body keeps learning: to ward off disease and adjust to temperature changes. Our brain takes in facts and remembers experiences. Our emotions ebb and flow[1].

A means of thriving in today's world
Human beings, like plants, are meant to grow. As we encounter the constant stream of developments around the globe, we evaluate new information and update what we know. Our world becomes our classroom. What we choose to notice and absorb becomes our curriculum. Through continuous learning, we grow intellectually, emotionally, and spiritually. We gain skills. We solve problems. We stay relevant, engaged, and productive.

Some of us learn by chance; others by command. Leaders learn by *choice*. We enjoy learning. We actively seek new ways to meet our needs and achieve our goals. We know we will solve more problems by putting in more effort. Leaders evolve and become lifelong learners[2]. In the world of work, only those who keep the mind sharp and the skills fresh will remain valuable and employable. Through learning, we uncover new opportunities and build new competencies. We gain confidence to make life or career changes. We become better workers and better family members. We fulfill and enrich our lives.

LEARNING IN LEADER DEVELOPMENT: THE LEARNING WEB OF BELIEF[SM]

Leadership and learning are indispensable to each other.
                                                    JOHN F. KENNEDY[3]

The first web of belief is learning: belief in our capacity to gain knowledge, integrate it into practice, and gain more advanced skills always and everywhere, throughout the career and life spans. Every day, discoveries add to our knowledge base. We learn new processes and adjust to new technologies. Leaders must believe we can always cope with the uncertainties, complexities, and challenges we encounter. Openness to new information and new perspectives contributes to our self-awareness and self-development. We note our strengths and weaknesses, value feedback, and make sense of realities emerging in our world[3]. We are always aware of how our experiences, our roles, and the people around us help us learn. We gain capacities for flexibility and complex cognitive processing. We find creative approaches to our leadership. Through the Learning Web of Belief, we develop personal, practical, and managerial wisdom.

REFLECTION ACTIVITY 3-1: THE LEARNING WEB OF BELIEF IN YOUR LIFE

Note ways you might be using the Learning Web of Belief[SM] in your life or work.

Aspects of the Learning Web of Belief[SM]	How do I practice this in life or work today?	How can I improve this in the future?
I believe in the capacity to gain knowledge.		
I integrate what I learn into practice.		
I continuously gain more advanced skills.		
I learn always and everywhere.		

UNDERSTANDING THE LEARNING WEB OF BELIEF[SM]: LEARNING IN LEADERSHIP TODAY

Humankind today has the capacity to create far more information than anyone can absorb, to foster far greater interdependency than anyone can manage, and to accelerate change far faster than anyone's ability to keep pace. Certainly, the scale of complexity is without precedent.
                                                    PETER SENGE[4]

Learning keeps us strong and capable as our realities evolve. A love of learning helps us embrace change. Through continuous learning, we gain confidence and self-efficacy. If we know how to learn, we easily gain technical and practical skills. We improve our reliability in the workplace because we are curious to seek opportunities and willing to take on challenges. We adopt new mindsets to improve our leadership of people and tasks. As we apply the Learning Web of Belief [SM], we become creative and wise[5]. We model for our peers and followers the benefits of knowing how to learn.

Our brain is wired for permanent learning
Biology and cognitive science explain how the brain collects and processes information. Our sensory memory hears, sees, smells, tastes, and feels information from our surroundings. These stimuli disappear from sensory memory in just a few seconds. Our short-term working memory selects or judges what the brain will process. In about 20 seconds, we choose what to store in long term memory. The information we encode to long term memory forms permanent neural connections in our brain. 95% of what we encode remains in our subconscious, waiting to be recalled[6].

The stimuli and conditions present when we learn something help make connections to retrieve that information. For example, have you ever been driving down the road and heard an old, familiar song on the car radio? Did it trigger a memory of a place or a time from long ago, including the people you were with and your emotions at the time? If so, you experienced how subconscious, long-term memories come back for active use. The same thing happens in situations needing our expertise or skill. For example, if you once learned CPR, you can quickly perform it when someone near you needs medical assistance.

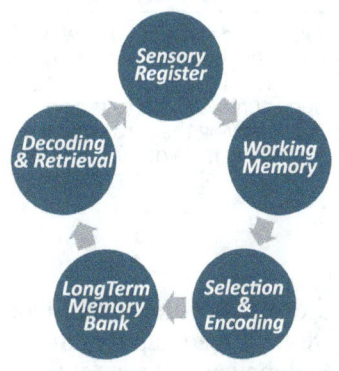

The brain goes through specific steps to process, retain, and retrieve what we learn. We gather information through our senses and can attend to only seven bits of information at a time. We decide what to focus on in working memory, then we convert that information to long term memory where it stays. Retrieving information can become automatic as we develop expertise in a particular skill or discipline. We retrieve "forgotten" information as we connect it back to when, or how, we encoded it.

Learning happens in steps and stages
Bloom's taxonomy is an instructional framework used by teachers to plan lessons and achieve learning objectives. It depicts how our learning of a topic progresses through different levels. We begin with the collection of simple knowledge then progress to deeper understanding. We apply what we learn to situations in work

and life. We analyze or compare new information to what we already know. We synthesize this knowledge to adjust meanings and make different connections.

At the highest level of learning, we evaluate or judge new information to create unique theories and innovative applications. This schema for learning is useful for anyone wanting to communicate information in any setting. Managers can use it to give direction. Team members can use it to create shared meaning. Parents can relay values and rules appropriate to their children's age and level of understanding. The chart below shows how it works[7].

The Levels of Learning in a Bouquet of Flowers

Level of Learning	Learning by a 3-year-old Child	Learning by an Adult
Knowledge	Sees something colorful in the yard.	Sees the child picking flowers in the yard.
Understanding	Learns these are called flowers and they grow in the warm weather.	Is glad the child is being creative, but wants the flowers to keep growing in the yard.
Application	Thinks they would be good to bring to their caretaker.	Receives the bouquet from the child and tells them they have done a very kind deed by giving a gift.
Analysis	Picks a few pink ones and green ones to bring in the house.	Sees the differences in colors and knows some are not flowers.
Synthesis	Sees there are also purple ones in the garden next door. Decides to add these to the bouquet.	Realizes there are weeds in the bouquet, as well as a few flowers from the neighbor's garden.
Evaluation	Decides the bouquet should be bigger and have more colors.	Does not want the weeds in the house; does not want the child wandering to a neighbor's yard.
Creativity	Goes back outside to find some yellow flowers in the grass. Excitedly brings the extra flowers into the house to add to the bouquet.	Takes the dandelions and weeds out of the bouquet before putting in a vase in the house. Uses the opportunity to teach a lesson about leaving the yard and taking something from others' property.

We learn through our stages of adulthood

We continue to learn throughout our life. Researchers provide several models for our development as adults. Erik Erickson gives us a roadmap for emotional and interpersonal (psychosocial) stages: the development of trust, autonomy, initiative, industry, identity, intimacy, generativity, and integrity. Levinson offers life stages or "seasons" of adulthood: early adult transitioning; forming a life structure; becoming one's own person; transitioning through midlife; and restabilizing in late adulthood. Kohlberg maps our moral development, as we discover our principles and live out our beliefs[8].

Several cognitive powers begin to evolve in adolescence and continue through adulthood: thinking about possibilities; applying reasoning to make sense of experiences and issues; metacognition, or thinking about our own thinking; thinking through complicated lenses; and realizing our beliefs are not absolute, or "black and white." We use these cognitive powers to understand self and others, as well as to develop leadership skillsets and mindsets. As we age, our brain processes information more slowly. Yet, our capacity for solving problems and dealing with complexity improves. Our collection of knowledge and experiences is the natural incubator for becoming smarter and wiser human beings.

The meaning and use of the Learning Web of Belief[SM] can change at different ages and stages ...

SELF-ASSESSMENT ACTIVITY 3-2: THINKING ABOUT YOUR ADULT DEVELOPMENT

Using the chart of adult ages and stages, circle the items which apply to you today.

Ages and Stages
An introduction to just a few of the guiding frameworks for adult development

Psychosocial Development[9]	The Evolving Mind[10]	Developmental Transitions[11]	The Seasons of Life[12]	Life Transitions[13]
Trust (hope) Autonomy (will) Initiative (purpose) Industry (competence)	Impulsive childhood	Dependence		Developmental Transitions
Identity (fidelity)	Imperial adolescent	Counter-dependence	Pre-adulthood	Planned Transitions
Intimacy (love)	Socialized	Independence	Early Adulthood	External Events
Generativity (care)	Self-authoring	Interdependence	Midlife Transition	Awakenings
Ego integrity (wisdom)	Self-transforming		Late Adulthood	

From what you circled above, describe your current stage of adult development:

We learn from our experiences everyday
When asked how they developed as leaders, a group of senior executives said they learned most of their leadership practices through experiences, not from schooling or training programs. A group of women leaders noted they learned via their own goal setting, critical thinking, and resourcefulness, not from classes or training on leadership topics[14]. Experiential learning is the process of learning from what we do and what we have done. Whether we are conscious of it or not, everything we experience has a lasting impact on our development. When we reflect on our current experiences to guide future action, we learn more quickly. We become transformative learners.

We learn via continuing education and training
Our formal learning, whether self-propelled or prescribed for us, continues throughout our life. To expand our repertoire, or become more valuable in the workplace, we enroll in training programs and certification courses. We seek new degrees. Using the internet, new knowledge and coursework is at our fingertips. We have the unprecedented opportunity to quickly access information we need, or to satisfy our curiosities. Academic and professional development is readily available in any learning style through websites, videos, podcasts, social media platforms, and artificial intelligence tools. We can seek data and facts we agree with, as well as information contrary to our beliefs. Leaders must use every option to continuously expand our knowledge, skills, and understanding.

We learn by observing and listening to others
Social learning is the process of observing others and adopting their behaviors as our own[15]. Leaders use all our senses to absorb new information from those around us. The people in our lives and our workplaces become our teachers and role models. By noting what others do and how they do it, we gather information about how to perform tasks or handle situations. Through listening and watching, we discover new options for our own leadership interactions, communications, and performance. We adopt new mindsets and behaviors. We also learn what *not* to do when we observe others.

REFLECTION 3-3: THINKING ABOUT OTHERS' ADULT DEVELOPMENT

List three to five adults in your life today. What life stage do you think they are in? Record some insights about how their adult development might be affecting their work and life.

An adult in my life today	Their stage of life	Insights on their adult development

We learn by expanding our comfort zone
Fear is the strongest human emotion and the greatest motivator of behavior. Fearfulness is the basis of low self-esteem, lack of confidence, and helplessness. Most of us fear the unknown. Taking on challenges and embracing new experiences means facing, then overcoming, fears. Trying something new builds skills and broadens our perspectives. Diverse experiences challenge us, but also inspire and motivate us[16]. As we gain new insights and build new skills, we improve our self-efficacy. We enjoy the process. We want to learn more. We live and work more confidently. We believe in ourselves. We unlock opportunities in our personal and professional lives.

We learn from significant life events
All humans deal with adversity in their lives. Significant life events, called crucibles, are opportunities for learning and transformation. Crucibles can be negative or traumatic occurrences such as health issues, loss of loved ones, career failures, or other setbacks. They can also be positive or challenging experiences in career and life, such as attaining a difficult goal or facing unexpected demands at work or at home. Developing leaders use significant life events to understand how they navigate adversity and change. We find meaning in these experiences and transitions. We note how we responded and adapted and celebrate what we learned. Through crucibles, leaders gain practical knowledge and insights to our identity and knowledge about our competencies. We increase our capacity to understand, cope with, and solve complex problems for the future[17].

ACTIVITY 3-4: A QUIZ ABOUT LEARNING ALWAYS AND EVERYWHERE

Think of two things you learned this week. Answer the questions below to check the breadth and depth of your learning.

Something I learned recently.	Where, how, from whom?	How did this add to my learning?	How did this change my understanding or beliefs about a person, situation, or problem?

LEADER COMPETENCIES & STYLES
WITHIN THE LEARNING WEB OF BELIEF[SM]

Adaptive, strategic, and complexity leadership competencies
Using the Learning Web of Belief [SM], adaptive leaders become aware of the emerging forces and changing conditions in their work and life. They get on the balcony, or look at the big picture from afar, to identify challenges and analyze their assumptions. They help their organizations generate ideas and make informed decisions. Strategic and complexity leaders adjust to the tensions in their environment. They use the learning web of believe to explore the effects of vulnerabilities and uncertainties and to organize creative responses[18].

Transformational leadership and change leadership competencies
The leadership of change requires learning to tune in to the environment and apply kaleidoscope, or multidimensional, thinking. Continuing to learn makes change leaders better at analyzing, problem-solving, and decision-making. Their novel ideas and innovative solutions support planning processes and the implementation of change[19]. Transformational leaders use intellectual stimulation to coach, teach, and mentor. Helping others learn improves their own understanding and creativity.

Authentic leadership, self-leadership, and emotional intelligence competencies
Self-leadership starts with knowledge of our capabilities. Leaders use learning to become aware of their skillsets, their mindsets, and their influence on others. Learning about their personal beliefs, values, and thinking processes helps leaders know who they are, where they are going, how they act, and why[20]. When individuals understand themselves, they develop better communication, decision-making, and relationship-building skills.

Leaders who believe in learning are self-motivated. They determine how to use, or not use, their strengths and weaknesses in work and in life. They learn how to improve their social skills and emotional intelligence. Authentic leaders learn to become realistic and humble about their capabilities and needs. They revise their behaviors based on new knowledge about who they are, what they believe, and what they can do. Being open to learning throughout the life and career spans deepens their perspectives. They gain critical thinking skills for clarity, accuracy, precision, and openness.

Servant leadership, connective leadership, and followership competencies
Connective leaders are lifelong learners who nurture followers and transform environments. The Learning Web of Belief [SM] drives them to listen, develop perspective, and be empathetic. Servant leaders and connective leaders learn about, and *from*, their followers. They encourage creativity and innovation by all[21].

HOW TO APPLY THE LEARNING WEB OF BELIEF^{SM} IN YOUR LEADER DEVELOPMENT

Understand your learning styles

Each of us must discover both how and when we learn best. The principle learning styles are visual, auditory, kinesthetic, and reading/writing. An individual often favors one style, but using several styles together is the best way to gain new knowledge and skills[22]. Identify and understand the ways in which you learn. Is your most effective learning style visual, auditory, hands-on, reading/writing, or a combination? Do you use different learning styles to master various types of information or skills? Is your learning affected by the context or situation you are in? What do you pay attention to with your short term working memory? How do you recall or retrieve information from your long term memory? Who are your teachers? Do you ask for feedback from coaches and mentors? What do you learn from your experiences? Does reflecting about your thoughts and actions help you change and improve?

SELF ASSESSMENT AND REFLECTION 3-5: HOW DO YOU LEARN?

Recall something you learned using each type of learning. You may have more than one example for some types of learning; you may have nothing to record for others.

WAYS WE LEARN	SOMETHING I LEARNED USING THIS METHOD
Visually	
Verbally	
Hands-On/Manually	
Reading/Writing	
From An Experience	
From Watching Someone	
From Listening to Someone	
From a Major Life Event	
From Schooling/Education	
From Overcoming a Challenge	
From Crossing a Boundary	
Other Ways I Learn	

Learn always and everywhere
Become an active and inquisitive learner for life. See, hear, feel, and understand what you are experiencing every day. Watch, and listen to, people around you. Make connections to your past knowledge and experiences. Expand your understanding of what you think, do, and feel. Empower yourself to receive information, process it, and construct new meanings and schemas.

Always make learning personal and relevant. Learn for yourself and think for yourself. The meaning and application of the same knowledge, behaviors, and emotions changes in different contexts and situations. Construe new interpretations to guide your future thinking. Your problem-solving and decision-making sharpens. Your emotional intelligence and interpersonal skills expand and improve. Developing as a leader is a lifelong process. When you adopt the Learning Web of Belief℠, your possibilities are endless.

Be keenly inquisitive
Asking questions is a powerful, yet humble, way to interact with others and learn from them. Deepen your learning by asking questions of yourself and others about current realities and future opportunities. To always be learning, ask questions such as: What is happening here? What am I hearing? What am I seeing? What am I feeling? What are others feeling? How does this situation connect to what I already know or what I already experienced? Use the answers to these questions to make sense of your experiences and extend your leadership skills.

Seek enrichment outside your comfort zone
Regularly seek information outside the narrow tunnel of your own life and work. Shed fear and trepidation about trying something unfamiliar. Challenge yourself to learn a new skill, take on a new hobby, accept a new role. When you persist through challenges your brain makes new connections. You stretch your knowledge and perspectives. You find new sources of satisfaction in life and work.

Network within your organization. Spend more time getting to know family members and friends. Explore other cultures. Talk to people who think and act differently than you. Seek diverse sources to learn about happenings beyond the bubble of your region, industry, and area of expertise. Travel! Begin by traveling to new places in your own community or industry. Extend your travel to other regions in your country and around the world. Understand how history impacts the present and the future. Make the world your classroom and strive to learn from all the people in it.

Reflect on your life experiences
Use the Learning Web of Belief℠ to understand the forces shaping your body, mind, and spirit. What, how, and from whom have you learned? Think about your childhood. Who were your friends in elementary school? In secondary school? What did you learn from them? What types of things did you do with them? Are you still connected with them? Why or why not? What activities or hobbies did you enjoy as a child? Did something, or someone, early in your life provide motivation to achieve? Did mentors, or significant others, affect your perspectives about schooling, ethnic differences, or lifestyle? Did a teacher along the way make you want to learn more about a subject? Did a good or a bad experience on a sports team influence how you act as

a team member or team leader? Did your successes (or failures) in school affect your belief in your ability to complete a task or set goals? Did the closest people in your life believe in you and support you, or did they make you doubt yourself? Did your religious upbringing (or lack of) influence your beliefs, values, or lifestyle? As you answer these questions, trace the development of your current leadership skills and mindsets.

Teach something to another
Teaching what you know to someone else involves the highest levels of learning: synthesis, evaluation, and creativity. You must prepare to teach by reviewing or re-learning a set of information. You frame, and re-frame, the material to make it relevant and meaningful to your students. You go back and check your own comprehension, analysis, and applications. You find new ways to explain so your learner will understand. As you teach, students may question your knowledge and experience, or ask for more information. This questioning drives you to refine your thinking and deepen your own understanding. You master the subject matter, and learn even more. You continue to develop intellectual and psychological powers. Take every opportunity to teach or explain what you know to others.

Seek feedback
How do you know what adjustments are needed and appropriate for your leadership? Your self-knowledge is limited without input from others. The only way to pinpoint your leadership needs is to combine your own knowledge with feedback. Get help from coaches, mentors, peers, and supervisors about what to change and how to improve. Ask questions about how you are doing: in your job, in your technical performance, in your teamwork, and in your leadership.

Ask what skills and mindsets to use in task- and people-related situations. The answers to these questions are powerful insights to your leader development. Resist the tendency to seek less feedback as you mature in your job role and in your life skills. Keep seeking feedback. Keep believing in personal and professional improvement. Be always and ever open to change.

Believe in a growth mindset
Your abilities support your effort, but hard work and a love of learning are more important. A growth mindset is belief that persistent effort and dedication will overcome challenges and achieve the best results[23]. Apply a growth mindset in all you do. Believe you can achieve. Devote more effort to solving problems and achieving goals.

Resist perfectionism and the need to be correct. Instead, admit you do not know all. Replace your pursuit of approval with a passion for more knowledge and understanding. Be positive about the transformational power of lifelong learning in your life and work. Your intrinsic motivation will heighten. Your engagement will deepen. The quality of your learning will improve because you are learning what you want to learn and what applies to you.

Make learning fun! Recognize how it improves your self-awareness, self-esteem, creativity, flexibility, resilience, and quality of life. Become interested in what you are learning and learn what interests you. The more you believe in your own learning, the more leadership mindsets and skillsets you will develop.

SELF ASSESSMENT AND REFLECTION 3-6: HOW TO USE THE LEARNING WEB OF BELIEF[SM]

Record your thoughts about how to use these tools for learning in your leadership. You may have more than one idea for an item. You may have no comments or ideas for others.

Learning Web of Belief[SM] Applications	How I Can Use This to Improve My Learning and Leadership
Understand my learning styles	
Learn always and everywhere	
Become keenly Inquisitive	
Go outside my comfort zone	
Reflect on my experiences	
Teach to others	
Seek feedback	
Adopt a growth mindset	

BEYOND THE INDIVIDUAL: THE LEARNING WEB OF BELIEF[SM] IN TEAMS & ORGANIZATIONS

Organizations only learn through individuals who learn.

PETER SENGE

Organizational learning is the process of creating, retaining, and transferring knowledge within an organization, with the goal to continue improving over time. Organizations and teams must embed a passion for learning in their cultures and processes. The pillars of a learning culture include personal mastery, shared mental models, shared vision, and team learning[24]. Learning must be in the organization's budget, then tracked, measured, and evaluated as an outcome.

Learning benefits every organization. Continuous training supports employees to learn new technologies, adopt more efficient processes, communicate competently, analyze problems, and adapt to change. Communications standards assure knowledge transfers up, down, and across the organization, and to future leaders. The process of benchmarking, or the study of best practices by competitors and/or companies in other industries, complements planning and creative thinking about products, services, and operations.

Employees make significantly more progress in learning and development if they are supported by compassionate role models and coaches. Leaders using the Learning Web of Belief ℠ encourage their people to take charge of their own training and development. They support outside education programs and encourage every worker to become a lifelong learner.

Commitment to learning becomes a cornerstone of health and welfare for an organization. Encouragement of learning develops loyal workers and fosters a positive work environment. Employee turnover is low because individuals experience personal and professional growth in their jobs. Front line workers and teams who are trained to embrace learning are more productive, more creative, and more empowered. They sincerely contribute to the organization's overall performance and results. In a learning organization, the community thirsts for knowledge to get things done and solve problems. People know it is okay to not have all the answers. Individuals and teams listen to each other, share knowledge, and learn from each other. They seek more information and offer better solutions. Interactions are respectful, enjoyable, and genuine. Everyone wants to learn more.

THE LEARNING WEB OF BELIEF℠ IN ACTION

Walt Disney: Artist, Entrepreneur, Entertainment Executive[25]

My brother was a kid all his life.
RUTH BEECHER DISNEY

In childlike fashion, Walt Disney never stopped learning how to provide magical experiences. He has inspired people of all ages to learn through enjoyment. As one of the most creative leaders of his time, Disney pushed the envelope of possibilities to invent new forms of animation and entertainment. Disney learned from his mistakes, starting with the failure of his first animation studio and his Oswald the Rabbit character. He taught other business leaders to develop teams of people who could coordinate efforts and teach each other. His vision for Disneyland and Disney World was not of amusement parks, but rather enchanting places where families could enjoy their time together. Using a growth mindset, he never stopped devoting effort to reach his dreams. He claimed Disneyland would never be finished, but always alive and growing. Walt Disney's enterprises continue through steps and stages, always developing new experiences for learning and enjoyment. Because of his dedication to learning, Walt Disney taught the world to imagine, innovate, and have fun.

John Wooden: UCLA Basketball Coach, Teacher, Author[26]

If you are through learning, you are through.
JOHN WOODEN

John Robert Wooden built his expertise and fame as an innovative basketball coach. Over his long career, he continuously adapted his methods to fit the game and his teams. However, Wooden did not consider coaching his most important work. His true mission was to propel his players to develop life skills and become lifelong learners. After studying the characteristics of successful leaders, he identified 25 behaviors for success. He trained individual players to focus on personal growth. He authored *The Pyramid of Success* to showcase his research. His book became the textbook in his locker rooms. Wooden's influence on learning communities transcends the basketball arena. His wise adages, called *Wooden-isms*, live on in education, sports, and business. *The Pyramid of Success* became one of the very early self-help guides. Considered timeless wisdom, it is still used for character and leadership education.

Taylor Swift: Songwriter, Singer, and Business Magnate[27]

Anything you put your mind to and add your imagination into can make your life a lot better and a lot more fun.
TAYLOR SWIFT

After learning about and loving country music, young Taylor Swift created her own music genre. She signed as a songwriter at age 14, then developed her own singing and performing talents. Many of her songs feature themes about learning, school, and remembering. She could not fit a college education into her busy schedule. Instead, she used a growth mindset to become a masterful businesswoman through her own learning and experience. As social media emerged and evolved, she became an expert user of its power to leverage her popularity. She built her brand, and, by age 32, became one of very few billionaire musician/performers. Taylor learns from trusted role models and advisors in marketing, branding, and merchandising. Teachers at all levels use her stories in a variety of school subjects. There is even a course on Taylor Swift at Harvard University. She continues to innovate and evolve because she knows she must keep reinventing herself and her music. She is only 30-something yet continues her learning to achieve her goals.

Richard Branson: Journalist, Entrepreneur, Adventurer[28]

You don't learn to walk by following rules; you learn by doing and falling down.
SIR RICHARD BRANSON

Richard Branson embraced learning and adventure at age six when he found his way home from a remote location. Dyslexia and nearsightedness caused him to drop out of school at 16 but did not subdue his inquisitive mind. He started a magazine focused on learning from young people's voices, then followed his passion for music to start a record store and recording company. Without a formal education, he challenged and changed the rules of several industries, including airlines, cruise lines, cargo delivery, and space travel. As he starts new endeavors, his vision is to question the status quo to create a product or service of great use. Sir Richard has never stopped breaking out of his comfort zone to explore and learn. He holds world records for crossing the oceans in a powerboat and hot air balloons. He was the first billionaire to travel to space in his own spacecraft. Branson motivates his employees to learn from their mistakes by delegating responsibility to them. He lives and works with a growth mindset, believing any frontier can be conquered with creativity and effort.

CONCLUSION

Learning is an essential component of life and leadership, or perhaps leadership and life are all about learning. There are infinite ways to learn always and everywhere: experiential learning, formal education, self-directed learning, mentoring, and reflective learning. Leaders using the Learning Web of Belief ℠ bestow great gifts upon their followers by teaching new skills and encouraging lifelong learning. Modeling a love for learning in your life and work is transformational for everyone you encounter. Keeping your mind youthful and active is a great source of fulfillment. Continuous learning improves your quality of life. It breeds success for your life and career. You will be proud, confident, satisfied, and healthier. Learning is part of the fun of life, so make it enjoyable.

ADDITIONAL RESOURCES

Ageless Body, Timeless Mind, Deepak Chopra, M.D., Three Rivers Press, 1993

Good Leaders Ask Great Questions, John C. Maxwell. Center Street Books, 2014

Immunity to Change: How to Overcome It and Unlock the Potential in Yourself and Your Organization, Robert Kegan and Lisa Laskow Lahey, Harvard Business Press, 2009

Leading in Complex Worlds, JoAnn Danelo Babour, Gloria J. Burgess, Lena Lid Falkman, and Robert M. McManus, Jossey Bass, 2012

Mindset, The New Psychology of Success. Carol S. Dweck, Ph.D. Ballantine Books, 2016

Magnificent Mind at Any Age, Daniel G. Amen, M.D. Three Rivers Press, 2008

New Passages, Mapping Your Life Across Time, Gail Sheehy, Ballantine Books, 1996

The 7 Habits of Highly Effective People, Stephen Covey. Free Press, 1989

The Fifth Discipline: The Art & Practice of The Learning Organization, Peter M. Senge. Doubleday, 1990

CHAPTER APPENDIX

The LEARNING Web of Belief[SM]	Competencies & Mindsets Developed Within Leadership Theories and Styles
Complexity/Strategic/Adaptive/Crisis Leadership Capacities	Adaptive capacity, innovator, absorptive capacity, managerial wisdom, cognitive complexity, identify organizational knowledge centers, transform via language and symbols, emergence, integrated understanding of organization, systems thinking, deep interpretive understanding, rule-based symbolic processing[29], get on the balcony[30]
Shared/Distributed/Relational Leadership Capacities	Inquiry, shared cognition, self-observation, contribute to others' development, self and other development, vicarious/mentor, shifting mental models, cognitive shifts, confront diverse ideas, high development and learning, master own tasks, analytical mindset, commitment to experimentalism, education and knowledge[31]
Authentic Leadership/Self Leadership/Emotional Intelligence Capacities	Self-awareness, awareness of values, cognitions, emotions, self-knowledge, self-diagnosis and understanding, identity development, individual skill and self-concept, adaptability, readiness for development, learning goal orientation, work with inner obstacles, experience, experimentation for improvement, expertise development, knowledge base development, automaticity, principle-level task expertise, successful adult development processes, involve others in learning, develop behavioral and self-regulatory skills in self and others, empowered creativity[32]
Change Leadership & Transformational Leadership Capacities	Continuous improvement, keep gaining, anchor change in the culture, articulate connections, evaluate systems and processes, sense of urgency, vision, continuous improvement, institutionalize change[33], tune in to the environment, use kaleidoscope thinking[34], intellectual stimulation, idealized influence[35], get the knowledge you need, focus on opportunities, not problems[36]

WORKING TOGETHER

A combined endeavor
by a small group of humans

is . . . Frustrating
Tedious
Time consuming
FUN

takes. . . Compromise
Control
Patience
Practice
Listening
REVERENCE

can. . . Forge new bonds
Create fresh perspectives
Nurture new ideas
Use all our talents
Solve problems

Bring about our best work
CHANGE THE WORLD

PAT O'CONNELL

CHAPTER 4

THE REVERENCE WEB OF BELIEF^{SM}

> Belief in acceptance and incorporation of the needs of everyone everywhere, with honor and awe of every person and all cultures' unique talents and contributions.

WHAT IS REVERENCE IN THE 21ST CENTURY?

An old virtue that is new again
Reverence for others was introduced by the Greek poets and philosophers to describe leaders who believe all people share a common humanity. The ancient Greeks used the concept of reverence as a basis for the introduction of democracy[1]. During the Middle Ages, church leaders encouraged reverence to venerate, respect, and honor religious and spiritual role models. In the thirteenth century, St. Francis of Assisi advocated reverence in his Canticle of the Creatures, encouraging respect and care for all creation. Reverence remains a major tenet of Franciscan teachings and values today[2].

The idea and practice of reverence re-emerged in the year 2000 when forward-thinking educators applied this ancient virtue to the teaching profession. They recommended teachers use reverence when working with students in the classroom. At the same time, philosophy and ethics scholars studied reverence as an interpersonal relations practice. They encouraged humans to rediscover reverence and apply it to daily life in the modern world. Reverence is enjoying new attention by scholars who believe it useful far beyond religion. They believe practicing reverence can create a sense of belonging to each other and our world[3].

Emphasizing awe, respect, honor, and esteem
Reverence is a concept and an action. It is one of the quiet virtues, underlying and subconscious. Philosophers define it as the capacity for awe and respect. The Greeks offered it as the opposite of pride, arrogance, and abuse of power. Reverence affirms life, emphasizes reconciliation, and is based in the ethic of love[4]. In human development, it molds character and guides action. Reverence balances our personal ambitions with a sense that we live and work in contexts more important than ourselves.

Focused on connections, not differences
Reverent individuals find beauty in the differences and diversities of people, places, and things across the globe. They are conscious of their own limitations and thus express awe and wonder about other humans. Leaders using this old, but new, concept navigate the infinite shades of values, beliefs, and social practices across societies. Leaders and individuals practicing reverence seek connections. They consider others' needs as important as their own. They believe involvement with diverse cultures will expand their perspectives.

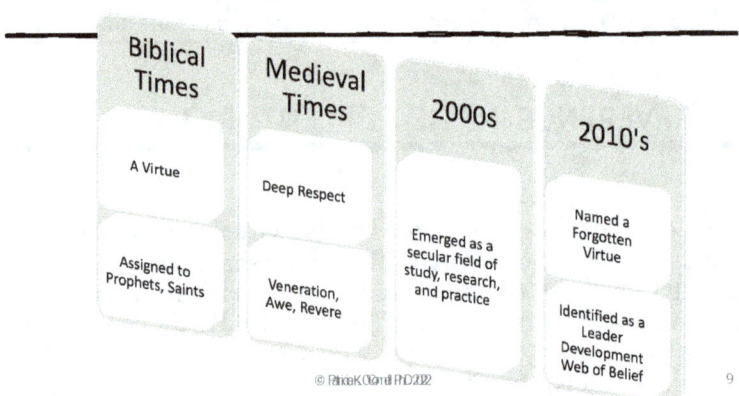

REVERENCE IN LEADER DEVELOPMENT: THE REVERENCE WEB OF BELIEF^{SM}

Leadership based in reverence is marked by admiration for every person and all creation. Reverent leaders welcome and include others' unique contributions and capacities. They forge relationships based on common values and are eager to learn about differences. They work side by side, equally, with people of all beliefs, talents, and identities, becoming global citizens who embrace multiculturalism. They develop emotional and cultural intelligence along with strategic and critical thinking skills. Reverence mindsets and skillsets are used in interpersonal relationships, communications, team membership, and team leadership. Practicing reverence promotes a sense of community and belonging.

Belief in reverence builds genuine and humble leaders with deep respect for followers. These leaders incorporate a diversity of perceptions and talents in teams and organizations. In time, they apply reverence to more complex situations in professional and personal settings. They learn to effortlessly manage the many complexities of human interaction.

Using the Reverence Web of Belief, leaders facilitate inclusive planning processes. Ethnic, religious, political, identity, and generational differences are embraced, then used to enrich decisions. Reverence among employees or team members helps generate more options and identify more opportunities. Problem solving becomes creative and robust. Leaders practicing reverence believe they can, and should, make connections with everyone everywhere. They enthusiastically explore the spaces beyond their own boundaries and borders. Instead of seeing differences, they see opportunities to bring people together. Those around them broaden their worldviews. Interpersonal connections grow stronger. Life and work become more interesting and enjoyable[5].

REFLECTION ACTIVITY 4-1: THE REVERENCE WEB OF BELIEF IN YOUR LIFE

Using the definition of the Reverence Web of Belief, note ways you might be using reverence in your life or work.

Aspects of the Reverence Web of Belief	How do I use or practice this in life or work today?	How can I use or improve this in the future?
I believe in acceptance and understanding of everyone everywhere		
I incorporate others' needs and identities		
I treat others with honor and awe		
I honor others' beliefs		
I am in awe of other cultures		

UNDERSTANDING THE REVERENCE WEB OF BELIEF[SM]: REVERENCE IN LEADERSHIP TODAY

Reverence is a virtue established long ago, yet it is clearly relevant to leadership today. Reverent leaders honor, respect, and accept what others bring to their work and life. They strive to understand differences. Instead of abusing power, they become connective, trusted, and even charismatic[6].

Our understanding of reverence begins at home
Humans are born with unadulterated love for everyone. An infant leaves the womb with an open and untainted mind, needing only to give and receive love[7]. Yet as children, we spend our first decade of life in a narrow and inward-focused

environment. We are raised in a specific place and time, within a unique family and community. The adults in our lives guide our thinking, our beliefs, and our actions. We are taught the meaning of "being good." We learn a set of manners, how to treat elders, and how to interact with siblings. We may be required to participate as a member of a neighborhood, a community, a church. From the combination of these early experiences, we develop a set of cultural beliefs and assumptions. This becomes our basis for comparing ourselves to the others in our world.

As toddlers, we begin to develop fears based on what we learned as right and wrong, good and bad, desirable and undesirable, proper and improper. We discover the consequences of our behaviors when those in charge praise us, reward us, or punish us. We learn to please those who love us most, but by doing so, we learn fear. We turn our power of love into worry and anxiety. As we struggle to meet others' expectations, we may begin to dislike ourselves. This starts our un-learning of love and reverence.

Leadership Case: Diversity Training or Reverence Training?

People across the world have striven for equality throughout history. Over the past century, nations and workplaces have welcomed individuals of extremely varied beliefs and backgrounds. To facilitate collaborative, productive, and creative performance, organizations established diversity, equity, and inclusion training programs. Some employees dread the continuous requirements for diversity training because they are naturally fearful of change and differences. In the 2020's, these policies are being questioned legally, as in the U.S. Supreme Court decision to disallow college admissions quotas based on race and income.

As world politics and organizations evolve, should we consider changing how we describe and teach collaborative productivity and creative interaction? Can the use of the terms "reverence" and "connection" better define the results we seek? Consider some 21st century definitions of reverence:

- Reverence allows us to balance our personal ambitions with the sense we are in a context larger and more important than ourselves[8].
- Reverence as a virtue has re-emerged in the 21st century, as it is beneficial to create a sense of community and belonging[9].
- Reverence provides the bridge and the basis for developing leaders to understand, embrace, and practice multiculturalism and connective leadership[10].

The term reverence evokes thoughts and feelings of awe, empathy, understanding, and consideration amongst individuals and teams with varied orientations and beliefs. Studies of reverence in leadership emphasize cultural mindfulness and considerate leadership[11].

What will you think about as you develop your leadership style: reverence or diversity? Can learning and practicing reverence in leadership and followership transcend differences and prevent polarization in our communities and workplaces? Can the use of alternative terminology to address challenges in the teaching and implementation of diversity, equity, and inclusion better bridge the gaps between us?

Our sense of reverence emerges from encounters
In adolescence, we become aware of the world beyond our home and family. We notice events outside our narrow existence. We seek new connections as part of our most important pursuit: our social development. We meet friends and visit households with unfamiliar traditions or beliefs. We may feel discomfort, disbelief, or confusion about how to respect these differences. We may, at first, be glad to return to our comfortable and secure home base. On the other hand, we may become curious about new ways of thinking and acting. We explore new realities. We may adjust our beliefs and understandings. We begin to form our unique thinking and identity.

Depending on how we are guided and schooled as young adolescents, we become either fearful or fascinated by new encounters and experiences. For healthy adolescent and adult development, we need to learn about concepts and practices beyond our home of origin. We must learn to compare and question. To become leaders of others, we must be comfortable, accepting, and respectful of unfamiliar ideas and traditions.

Our capacity for reverence grows through experiences
As young adults we enter post-secondary school or join the workforce. We undergo training and build career skills. As we venture to independence, some young adults begin to see the world through new lenses, becoming open and respectful. Others retreat to comfortable places and familiar beliefs. To develop reverence, we must seize, and savor, a broad range of experiences. Through exposure to differences, we expand our comfort zone to include the many variations of people and places, near and far. We come to understand our own worldview and how it affects others. We establish our unique identity and presence in the world[12].

Using reverence, we cross boundaries
We all carry conscious and subconscious biases developed from our sphere of influence. These prejudices inform our thoughts, behaviors, and decisions as adults and leaders. Inclusion of others means accepting visible, and invisible, differences in religions, politics, lifestyles, learning styles, ethnicities, experiences, values, thoughts, and so much more. We find these visible and invisible differences across the globe, as well as in our own families, communities, and workplaces.

Reverence lessens our predispositions as we seek to understand the what, where, and why of our diversities. We open our minds and hearts to diverse ideas and behaviors. We work effectively with varied cultural and communication styles. We find there are as many approaches to living and working happily and successfully as there are people in our world. We accept everyone everywhere.

Leadership Case: Are Tattoos Acceptable for Professionals[13]?

Many parents in Western cultures, including the United States, forbid their children to get a tattoo, thinking they will not be accepted by future employers. Visible tattoos are traditionally restricted in military, airlines, medical professions, acting, teaching, law enforcement, and business professions. Yet, tattooing was practiced in prehistoric times and in ancient Greek and Egyptian civilizations. In India, Africa, Pakistan, and the Middle East, tattooing emerged as a way to naturally cool the body in hot, dry climates. Tribal peoples in Polynesia, India, and New Zealand attach social symbolism and cultural identity to body art. Tattoos in Asian cultures are used to express social or religious status. In Eastern indigenous cultures, tattoos are considered important art forms. Today, body art is finding its way into mainstream Western culture. In 2023, 40% of U.S. adults had at least one tattoo. The "ink revolution" is becoming a form of personal expression and art, as it has been in many cultures since ancient times. Tattooing across the globe is a $50 billion dollar industry. To accommodate this growing practice across generations, business organizations have official policies about the visibility and content of tattoos. Employees and interviewees, especially in the United States, must research the acceptability of tattoos by their employers. Yet, history and archaeology show that banning tattoos is irreverent to many cultural traditions. The ancient practices of body art are also contemporary and universal!

What do you believe about the appropriateness of tattoos? What are the norms and expectations for body art in your profession and in your place of employment?

REFLECTION 4-2: THE ARRAY OF PEOPLE IN YOUR LIFE

Think about people in your life or work who have different beliefs or identities from your own. Make a note on how you can better interact with them and what you can learn from them.

People I Know with Different Identities or Beliefs	How I Interact With Them	What I Can Learn from Them

Reverence is about connections, not differences
Leaders practicing reverence appreciate the value and worth of our fellow human beings. We approach everyone we encounter in work and life as a person with sincere beliefs and aspirations. We know that hidden within their outer shell is someone who simply wants the best for themselves, their loved ones, and their community. We seek to uncover the common values, shared experiences, and challenges to face together.

Reverence in leadership is leadership with heart. Instead of considering differences as walls and barriers, we see diversity as a bridge to new knowledge and experiences. We observe the array of beliefs and customs across the street as well as across the globe. We work to understand others. We explore common needs and shared interests. As we discover what we agree on, we change our discomfort and fear to honor and admiration.

In our personal lives, reverence is acceptance of our family and community members, knowing they are growing, changing, and marching to the beat of their own drum. Our closest friends and relatives may follow paths and adopt beliefs different from our own. When we treat them with reverence, we maintain our relationships and find ways to enrich our connections. Leaders who believe in reverence know the power of networking and building relationships in the workplace. We admire others' talents and capabilities. We join with co-workers and lead teams to maximize productivity. We include others in problem solving and decision making. We enjoy working together.

Leadership Case: Thinking and Feeling Across Borders

> The five core emotions of joy, sadness, fear, anger, and disgust expand to thousands of words and descriptions across cultures and languages. Certain individuals and cultures express emotions and interact easily and frequently. Others do not. This is just one example of the differences pulling us apart, or creating disrespect, when we do not understand others' traditions.
>
> *In your family, or at your workplace, which emotions are acceptable to express to others?*

Reverence is humble but powerful
Reverence is the antidote to hubris or using power in a way that hurts people[14]. When we practice reverence, we are quiet listeners and humble observers. We understand our own limitations and want to tap into the talent and ideas of others. We spend time and effort understanding people who, at first, seem different from us. We seek education about culture, history, and current events. We become comfortable in unfamiliar places and with others' invisible traits. We do not force our ideas or our traditions on others. Reverence requires careful and active listening. Perhaps reverence is listening. Surely, listening is a sign of our humility.

Practicing reverence is a lifelong challenge
Humans are naturally egocentric. Without knowing it, we become self-centered thinkers with limited understanding of others. Our fears and insecurities feed selfishness and unwillingness to accept and include others. We choose self-preservation and fill our own needs versus considering others' rights and needs. We use narrow-minded thinking to justify our personal beliefs and behaviors. We want to judge and control others' actions or thinking, all due to our own fear of change and fear of being wrong. As we travel through life, we must fight the natural tendency to retreat into our narrow world and close our hearts to others. Our spirits must become rooted in reverence.

SELF-ASSESSMENT 4-3: A PROFILE OF YOUR IDENTITY

Fill in the blanks to describe your background and identity traits. Indicate where and how you acquired these beliefs or traits. You may not have answers for every item.

Visible aspects of my culture and identity	When/Where/From whom I learned or acquired this
Family:	
Ethnicity:	
Gender:	
Nationality:	
Geographic Region:	
Language:	
Physical Appearance:	
Disabilities:	
Personality Traits:	
Other:	

Invisible aspects of my culture and identity	When/Where/From whom I learned or acquired this
Education Level:	
Socioeconomic Status:	
Religion/Religious Beliefs:	
Political Beliefs:	
Gender Identity:	
Health Conditions:	
Marital Status:	
Other:	

LEADER COMPETENCIES & STYLES WITHIN THE REVERENCE WEB OF BELIEF[SM]

Social, emotional, and cultural intelligence competencies

With respect and honor for others, leaders increase their capacity to form relationships, solve problems collaboratively, and work in teams. As they use the Reverence Web of Belief, leaders gain social intelligence competencies including conversational skills, understanding of social rules, and adapting to others' behaviors[15]. They develop emotional intelligence and empathy to sense others' emotions, imagine what they are thinking or feeling, and understand the reasons for their behaviors. Cultural intelligence and cross-boundary competence develop as leaders experience new geographies and interact with people of diverse beliefs, traditions, and lifestyles.

Leaders who believe in reverence listen patiently and actively without judgment. They adopt verbal and non-verbal skills for communicating with respect and esteem. They cooperate and collaborate with others. They develop critical thinking skills to seek depth, breadth, accuracy, and clarity when asking questions and solving problems. They get to know the people in their life and work, make connections, and positively influence followers' performance.

Transformational leadership, adaptive leadership, complexity leadership, crisis leadership, and change leadership competencies

Transformational leaders use reverence for individual consideration, idealized influence, connection, and trust in team members[16]. They are humble and open to others' input. They build collective identity and improve teams' efficacy. They learn the power of constructive dialogue and listening, then facilitate productive decision-making and positive follow-through. They develop charismatic and engaging relationships. By modeling reverence, leaders help peers and followers expand their understanding, acceptance, and inclusion of a broad array of ethics and emotions.

To lead through complexity, reverent leaders are facilitators and coordinators focused on global needs. Adaptive leaders who practice reverence take a step back and observe the bigger picture of the environment and problem, then empower followers to contribute ideas and make decisions. They develop networks, enrich connections, and enable productive results from their teams[17]. Change leaders use reverence when they tune into their surroundings, empower others, form coalitions, and make everyone a hero. They are open to others' needs and perspectives. They remove obstacles and involve everyone's talents. Followers commit and contribute to lasting change initiatives because leaders listen to their ideas.

Authentic leadership, connective leadership, considerate leadership, team leadership, and servant leadership competencies

As they accept each person's unique talents and listen to their input, authentic leaders develop transparent relationships with peers and followers. They honor, value, and appreciate others not just for what they do, but also for who they are and what they believe. Considerate leaders build trusting relationships with followers. They manage diverse teams with compassion. Servant leaders practice reverence when they put followers ahead of themselves, show empathy, listen actively without judgment, encourage diversity of thought, and build community[18].

REFLECTION EXERCISES 4-4: VALUE SYSTEMS BY GENERATIONS: LOOKING FOR COMMON GROUND

Much is studied about differences in generations, and we often struggle with understanding each other and working together. Complete this table by thinking about the values of people you know from different generations. Use yourself in the column for your own generation.

VALUES	A Baby-Boomer in my life (1946-1964)	A Gen X-er in my life (1965 – 1980)	A Millennial in my life (1981-1996)	A Gen Z-er in my life (1997-2012)
Their personal values				
Their workplace values				

How alike or different are we across the generations?

HOW TO APPLY THE REVERENCE WEB OF BELIEF[SM] IN YOUR LEADER DEVELOPMENT

Believe in unique contributions by everyone everywhere
To become reverent in leadership, consider every fellow human as a unique and complex individual, shaped by a society, a culture, and a family. Find the good, the fun, and the fascination in other people. Know you can learn something everywhere you go and from everyone you meet. Believe they can make a meaningful contribution to your life and work. Listen to everyone's ideas to uncover new opportunities and creative options for getting things done. The more diverse perspectives we apply to solve a problem, the better and more effective the solution will be.

Move from judgment to observation, forgiveness, and acceptance
Each of us develops a personal code of conduct with clear expectations for ourselves and others. We label unacceptable actions as wrong, bad, hurtful, or improper. Judgment becomes a habit and is our first reaction to any encounter. We judge ourselves (guilt), and we judge others (resentment). Our rush to judgment harms current relationships and impedes new relationships[19]. We deprive ourselves of expanding our awareness and our opportunities. To practice reverence, become aware of your tendency to quickly compare or judge another based on what you would do or think. When you encounter someone with a behavior or an idea unpleasant to you, stop before you start. Do not act

or react, verbally or nonverbally. Calmly and simply observe. Be open to what you see, hear, and feel. Ask yourself why you feel annoyed, uncomfortable, or confused. Is this behavior or idea foreign to you? Is it something you would not do? Is it something you were taught not to do or say? Or is it something you do not understand?

Make a conscious effort to take the other person's perspective. Is their behavior related to how they were raised, their inborn personality, or their ambitions? Is there something in their life causing difficulty? Are they just having a bad day? Ask yourself what you can learn about them or yourself from this interaction. Change the picture in your mind of what you think *should be*. Accept yourself as you are, and accept others as they are: not perfect, but fellow human beings, trying to live their life in the best way they know how.

Are you holding a grudge against anyone in your life today? Take a moment to think about why. What caused the rift? Is this still an issue? Consider the circumstances or current life issues of the other person. Is it time to let it go and begin to forgive? Think about your judgments and opinions from three to five years ago. If you do not remember what they are, you have already let them go. If you do remember, think about what has changed, and what you have learned from another's opinions and beliefs.

If your reverence for others has grown, you will observe and understand people and situations with more acceptance and less judgment. You will honor each person's strengths and weaknesses. You will enjoy their idiosyncrasies. You will find ways to incorporate the multitude of differences among us to solve problems more readily. You will be more creative and innovative in your life and work.

Use empathy to expand your critical thinking skills

Empathy is vital to reverence. It includes listening to another, reflecting on their thoughts and emotions, and trying to feel what they are feeling. Instead of critique or lack of concern for others' ideas or behaviors, listen with compassion and an open mind. Do not react until you better understand their situation. Note the tone, the cadence, and the body language of others during communication. Uncover the meanings and emotions behind their words. Be pleasant, caring, and humble in response to another's needs and moods. Seek perspective, depth, clarity, and reasons behind what you see and hear.

Leadership Case: Pursuing the Contrary

> I once met a Fortune 500 CEO who wanted to better understand his markets and his people. On international flights, he did not catch up on work. Instead, he spent time reading or listening to information opposite from his own knowledge and belief system. This made him approach his organization and his customers with empathy, acceptance, and reverence. He gained the ability to lead across global markets and diverse cultures. He opened his thinking, became more innovative, and solved complex problems. His company grew and successfully served all its stakeholders.
>
> *How and when can you access information outside your personal belief system to expand your perspectives?*

Make connections and re-connections
At the heart of reverence is connection. When we connect with another, we observe them and learn from them. Practice making connections every day. Say hello to people you pass in the hallways, on the street, in the gym, in the grocery store, in the park, or while walking your dog. Smile. Wish them a good day. Wonder and imagine who they are, what their talents are, and where their goodness lies. If you get the chance, ask some questions to develop a stronger bond.

As we move through life and career, we experience bumps in the road with people in our world: family, co-workers, team members, managers, or fellow volunteers. When we disagree with someone, we become uncomfortable. We tend to stop the conversation, retreat into our corner, and avoid further contact or dialogue. We find ourselves criticizing the other person, their ideas, or their behavior. When this happens, stop yourself from becoming frustrated, confused, or disagreeable. Try a more peaceful tactic. Simply spend more time with that person. Change the topic or the venue. Find a way to make a positive connection and discover common ground. Find shared likes and dislikes. Engage in a fun activity together. Once you have a better connection, you may find you enjoy the person and can overlook differences. Share information to understand each other's perspectives and points of view. Often, you will discover the disagreement is not as serious as you first thought. You will mend a fence, and might even make a new friend, by practicing reverence!

Pursue relationships and experiences outside your comfort zone.
Our background, our fears, and our need for security often cause us to remain within the confines of our day-to-day world. With all we have on our to-do lists, it is easy, even natural, to simply stay in our cozy and predictable spaces. Reverence involves actively seeking diverse information and experiences. This takes conscious effort and persistence.

To learn about reverence, reach out to new people, and go to new places. Listen to ideas and opinions different from your own, without judgment or criticism. Take in what is strange or novel. Ask questions. Gather information. Analyze these inputs. Consider your observations and data as pieces of a puzzle not yet assembled. Applaud yourself for stretching the borders of your comfort zone.

All through life and career, challenge yourself to think and understand what is "outside your box." Each time you go beyond your boundaries, you learn something new. You gain confidence and energy. You understand more and accept new realities. As you widen your lens, your zone of comfort extends broader and deeper. You will celebrate the experiences and people you find. You will become more comfortable with being uncomfortable.

Develop skills for dialogue and constructive conversations
Practicing reverence is about connective communications: listening, exchanging information, sharing meaning, and expressing understanding of ideas different from our own. Working through what is being said, and processing new ideas requires constructive dialogue. In today's verbal and information-filled world, stopping to think before we speak is a lost skill. When in conversation, give and take. Slow the pace. Moments of silence are okay. Allow pauses. Responses, reactions, and answers do not have to be instant. Learn to express

your own beliefs and ideas clearly and objectively. Become aware of your choice of words, voice tone, volume, cadence, and body language. These cues and nonverbals are critical to both listening and speaking reverently. Aim for mutual understanding and respect.

There are many resources available for learning to effectively address conflict and differences. Take a course, listen to podcasts, or invest in guidebooks about constructive communication, negotiation, conflict management, and assertiveness. Before an important dialogue or critical conversation, review the steps for stating your needs, getting to agreement, and finding win-win solutions[20]. Learn how to receive and respond to negative feedback. Learn how to offer constructive feedback to others.

Reverent and successful communication between humans requires continuous learning and constant practice. Prepare for all conversations, especially difficult ones. After a dialogue, reflect on what you said and how you were received. Before you respond or react to a conflict, think first. Be empathetic. Develop a plan to resolve issues and improve understanding. Make a note about how you can improve your next communication. Transform the struggle into an opportunity to strengthen a relationship.

Travel the world: figuratively and literally
To travel is to live.
    HANS CHRISTIAN ANDERSON

Throughout life, connect with new people and new places. You do not have to go far to find people to learn from. The best way to expand the mind and the heart for reverence is to travel outside your home, your city, your state, your country, and your continent. The neighbor next door, a teammate at work, and your own relatives have diverse beliefs and habits. Learn from them. Discover the contributions they make to your life and career. Interact with people who live and work in different geographies. Attend a church service of a new or unfamiliar denomination.

Invest time and money to learn the practice of reverence. Travel abroad. When traveling, be a humble observer of the people and culture, and an eager wanderer of the geography. Interact with local people. Talk about life, family, hopes, and dreams. Exchange stories and information about the differences in your lives, your daily experiences, the weather, sports, habits and customs, rules and regulations. Stop, listen, and learn. Be respectful and accepting. Break bread together or have Three Cups of Tea[21]. Find common ground. Make lasting connections. Discover and discuss the basic human values global citizens share. Never stop travelling near and far.

Leadership Case: The Power of Connecting Across Boundaries

As I began the first webs of belief research project, I spent the summer in Europe. The trip combined study, presentations, teaching, and touring in six different countries. At that point, four webs of belief and their titles had emerged. However, the fifth web had no name: it involved balance, reflection, observation, and rest. I searched high and low for a term to combine these concepts. While in a wine café in Saint-Germaine des Pres, Paris, I started a conversation with a teacher from St. Thomas, sitting at the table next to mine. As we shared stories, I relayed my dilemma about naming the last

> web of belief. She immediately exclaimed, "There is a French term for that: flâneur!" She explained the origin and meaning of the word. Flâneur (pronounced flah-nure') became the fifth web of belief. That evening, I crossed the boundaries of my comfort zone, ventured out, and connected with a stranger. My life and my work were transformed. This is only one of the countless and incredible connections I have made during my travels to all seven continents.
>
> *Recall a time when you connected with a stranger or met someone new. What did you learn or discover? What fascinated you about them?*

BEYOND THE INDIVIDUAL: THE REVERENCE WEB OF BELIEF[SM] IN TEAMS & ORGANIZATIONS

Organizations today must navigate a complex, flattened, and uncertain world, marked by globalization and technological revolution. Throughout human history, small groups have gotten things done and nurtured individuals to survive and advance. Likewise, the most important tasks of an enterprise (strategizing, improving, innovating) cannot be accomplished by individuals alone. They require collaboration by globally competent, connective teams. As these teams form and go through stages, using reverence encourages participation and constructive dialogue.

Leaders with reverence accept and honor the panorama of diversities they encounter in co-workers, customers, and suppliers. They show openness, understanding, and appreciation of team members' many identities. When an organization believes in reverence, individuals contribute the best of their talents and skills because they are accepted, included, and respected.

Reverence is crucial in decision making. Whether on the production line, with customers, or in support functions, everyone must contribute ideas and needs. Organizations subscribing to the Reverence Web of Belief take time to consider all options, build consensus, and create shared meaning[22]. When change is needed, the culture of awe and respect leads to robust implementation of strategic goals. Organizations practicing reverence encourage the hearts of individuals and teams[23]. When challenges or failures occur, practicing reverence is about finding solutions, not pointing fingers or addressing blame. Problems and errors become learning experiences. People are not afraid to try again. Everyone extends their comfort zones and learns new skills.

Organizations who believe in the value of contributions by everyone everywhere fully utilize talents and reduce turnover. Innovation and creativity abound. Cooperation and cohesiveness develop. People get things done together. Communications improve. These are the places where individuals and groups achieve goals seemingly beyond their reach or their capabilities. Why? Because employees feel valued for their contributions. People give their all without fear of rejection, reprisal, or of not being heard. The culture becomes positive and optimistic. High-performing team members enjoy each other and have fun at work. People work together to get more done, and all succeed[24].

ASSESSMENT EXERCISE 4-5: REVERENCE SKILLS & MINDSETS

Record your thoughts about how to use these tools for reverence in your leadership. You may have more than one idea for an item. You may have no comments or ideas for others.

Reverence Skills and Mindsets	How I Can Use This to Improve my Reverence and Leadership
Believe in everyone's unique contributions	
Move from judgment to acceptance and forgiveness	
Use empathy	
Make connections and re-connections	
Pursue experiences outside my comfort zone	
Improve dialogue and constructive conversation skills	
Travel the world figuratively and literally	

THE REVERENCE WEB OF BELIEF[SM] IN ACTION

Oprah Winfrey: Television Show Host, Producer, Author, Actor[25]

Your legacy is every life you've touched.
Feel everything with love, because every moment you are building your legacy.
Living in the moment brings you a sense of reverence for all of life's blessings.
OPRAH WINFREY

From a background of poverty and abusive experiences, Oprah Winfrey vowed to inspire people across the globe to dream big and change the world for the better. She uses her advanced communications skills to help others solve life problems and develop life skills. Oprah is a master of questioning, and she is considered one of the world's best interviewers because she listens three times more than she talks. In over 37,000 interviews, she has explored the needs and challenges of almost everyone everywhere. She makes people feel special and guides them to understand each other. She has used her own weaknesses and mistakes to teach respect, honor, and awe for people of all beliefs and cultures across the globe. Leaders can learn dialogue and constructive communications from this humble, yet powerful, role model. In 2021, Forbes named her the most influential Woman of Diversity to continue to watch and learn from. Oprah Winfrey embodies leadership based in connection and heart.

Muhammad Yunus: Economist, Human Rights Champion, Social Entrepreneur[26]

Poverty is an artificial, external imposition on a human being; it is not innate in a human being. And since it is external, it can be removed. It is just a question of doing it.

MUHAMMAD YUNUS

Muhammad Yunus of Bangladesh traveled the world as a boy scout. While in college, he went outside his comfort zone to visit a poor village. There, he discovered the inspirational power of granting very small loans to individuals without their own resources. When he loaned $27 of his own money to villagers starting a business, they made a profit and advanced economically. His Grameen bank helped reduce world poverty by connecting people to each other and to the resources they needed. Muhammad's vision was to teach people across cultures and civilizations financial principles to help themselves. His Social Business Global Initiatives serves over 100 underdeveloped countries. Yunus received the 2006 Nobel Peace Prize as the father of microfinance and microcredit with awe for the underprivileged. Yunus is now involved across several continents and at the United Nations, promoting sustainable and equitable development and human rights. Yunus believes poor communities can succeed and improve their quality of life. He has changed the way the world thinks about developmental economics. After a period of uprising and violence in 2024, he was chosen as interim leader of Bangladesh by a committee of military, civic, and student leaders.

Mother Teresa of Calcutta: Servant Leader, Community Organizer, Saint[27]

Do small things with great love.

MOTHER TERESA

Teresa Bojaxhiu never let go of the natural love she was born with. Her mother taught her compassion for all. She dedicated her life in India to honor and serve people in sickness and poverty regardless of their race, age, or financial status. Teresa established The Missionaries of Charity, a community of nuns with a vow to give wholehearted free service to the poorest of the poor. In her ministry, she connected with one person at a time and put their needs before her own. Mother Teresa became world renowned for her selflessness as she honored all those in need. She is canonized as Saint Teresa of Calcutta. Her mission of reverence lives on, with 5,750 sisters and brothers serving in 120 developed and developing countries as of 2023. She remains a symbol of love and respect for all humankind.

Shonda Rhimes: Screen Writer, Television Producer, Social Change Agent[28]

The narrative of human life is most beautiful when told truthfully and without boundaries.
SHONDA RHIMES

Shonda Lynn Rhimes writes and produces television dramas that champion inclusion. She became one of the most influential screenwriters in television history by crafting lead roles for the most diverse characters ever represented on television. From Grey's Anatomy to Scandal to Bridgerton, she chronicles every type of human being, hoping audiences will connect with them and understand them. Through her characters, she has created awareness and advocated reverence for peoples without a voice. Her work reaches audiences of every belief and culture and opens dialogue about controversial issues. Shonda's trailblazing work breaks down barriers as her characters share their stories on the screen.

CONCLUSION

As we gain skills and mindsets for reverence, we expand our perspectives and value everyone's diversity. We incorporate and appreciate others' contributions. Individuals, teams, and organizations do not need to teach diversity or focus on differences. Equity and inclusion come naturally and effortlessly via our awe and honor for others. If we believe in reverence, we become humble about our own beliefs and traditions. We accept and respect other cultures. We better understand our own identity. Reverent individuals, teams, and organizations fearlessly explore unfamiliar beliefs and behaviors. Seeking experiences and relationships outside our boundaries becomes enjoyable. We build critical thinking and communications skills to get things done in our personal and professional arenas. We travel the world without leaving home. When we do travel the globe, we are filled with wonder and broaden our perspectives. We make connections with our fellow humans, and we find they are more like us than we first believed.

ADDITIONAL RESOURCES

American Citizen, Global Citizen. Mark Gerzon, Harvard Business Press, 2010
Creating Effective Teams. Susan A. Wheelan. Sage, 2010
Good Leaders Ask Great Questions, John C. Maxwell. Center Street Books, 2014
Growth Mindset, The New Psychology of Success. Carol S. Dweck, Ph.D. Ballantine Books, 2016
Inclusive Conversations. Mary-Frances Winters. Berrett-Koehler, 2020
Leading through Conflict. Mark Gerzon, Harvard Business Press, 2006
Peace, Reconciliation, and Social Justice Leadership in the 21st Century. H. Eric Schockman, Vanessa Hernandez, Aldo Boitano. Emerald, 2019.
Reconcilable Differences: Connecting in a Disconnected World. Dawna Markova, Ph.D. & Angie McArthur. Spiegel & Grau, 2017.
Servant Leadership Roadmap. Cara Bramlett, PA-C. carabramlett.com, 2023
Teams That Thrive. Ryan T. Hartwig & Warren Bird. InterVarsity Press, 2015
The Art of Forgiveness, Lovingkindness, and Peace. Jack Kornfield. Bantam, 2002
The Secret of Teams. Mark Miller. Berrett-Koehler, 2011
The Servant. James C. Hunter. Crown Businesss, 1998
The Study and Practice of Global Leadership. Gama Perruci, Emerald Publishing, 2022
The World is Flat 3.0: A Brief History of the Twenty-first Century. Thomas L. Friedman, Picador Publishing, 2007
Three Cups of Tea: One Man's Mission to Promote Peace…One School at A Time. Greg Mortensen and David Oliver Relin, Viking Penguin, 2006.
Use Your Difference to Make a Difference. Tayo Rockson, Wiley, 2019
You're Not Listening. Kate Murphy. Celadon Books, 2019

CHAPTER APPENDIX

The REVERENCE Web of Belief℠	Competencies & Mindsets Developed Within Leadership Theories and Styles
Complexity/Strategic/ Adaptive/Crisis/Executive Leadership Capacities	Enable correlation, manage and develop networks, focus on global interactions, enable conditions for adaptive interaction, engage across boundaries, influence org behavior, credibility, direction, facilitator, monitor, coordinator, broker, director, provide encouragement, enabling leadership, function effectively in social systems, productive well-being of one agent or aggregate is dependent on the productive well-being of others, followers participate in idea generation and decision making, encourages[29], socially interactive engagement, inclusion, mobilize collective action, empathetic, drive toward actionable intelligence[30], uplift others, socially interactive engagement, empathy[31], think & say "we" not "I"[32]
Shared/Connective/ Servant/ Team/Leadership and Followership Capacities	Team orientation, conjoint agency, interdependence, trusteeship, spontaneous collaboration, coordination, cross-hierarchy, self-managed work teams, co-leadership, participative goal setting & decision making, connectivity, followership, team trust, team efficacy/potency, team commitment, negotiate shared understanding, relationships, building bonds, friendship, mutual growth, empower, enable, leader-member exchange, universal values[33], encourage the heart[34], empathetic, collaborative, networkers, and nurture followers[35], agree on roles, norms & individual differences, create shared values, shared meaning, accept and understand the influence of others, reflect on leaders, observation[36]
Authentic Leadership/ Self Leadership/Emotional Intelligence Capacities	Relational transparency, positive social exchanges, collective psychological capital, positive, other-directed emotions, self-transcendent values[37], positive social exchanges, compassion, heart38, balancing me with we, look beyond yourself , understanding when to decide, when to consult subordinates or peers and bring them into the decision-making, social skills, empathy, expose yourself to different people, different social situations, see others' perspectives, social intelligence, interpersonal skills, emotional skills, prudence, helping conflicting parties to collaborate, win-win outcomes[39]
Change Leadership & Transformational Leadership Capacities	Build coalitions, make everyone a hero[40], empower, enable, build coalition of committed people around a common opportunity, achieve the goal together, clear the way for people to innovate, work more nimbly across silos, energize volunteers[41], individualized consideration, idealized influence, intellectual stimulation, inspirational motivation[42]

KEEP ON TREKKING

Continue on your path.
Endure the race.
Find joy in the journey.
Rejoice and be blessed
by what you create and find.
Your view of life
will be brilliant
when you cross your finish line.

PAT O'CONNELL

CHAPTER 5

THE PURPOSE WEB OF BELIEF℠

> Belief and engagement in personal mission, passion, and contributions to others in the form of roles, work, and service throughout the career and life spans

WHAT IS PURPOSE IN THE 21ST CENTURY?

Finding meaning in what we do
Philosophers and religious leaders, from Aristotle and Plato to St. Augustine and John Dewey, have studied human purpose over the ages. Purpose is the persona setting intentions and striving to accomplish them. Believing in a purposeful life is knowing there are aims to our actions and ways to fulfill our needs, beliefs, and desires[1]. This creates a deep sense of self-worth and contributes to the common good. When our purpose aligns with our concept of who we are and what we value, we find life meaningful. We experience happiness and satisfaction.

A basis for motivation from within
Leaders use purpose in their lives to control behaviors and adapt to new circumstances. If they believe their life and work matter, they become self-directed and internally driven toward accomplishment. They generate energy to set and achieve significant goals. They want to complete tasks, even if they are not fully enjoyable[2]. In our complex and uncertain world, challenging work becomes a source of motivation and flow.

A path to well-being in work and life
Experiencing life and work as meaningful is associated with well-being. Leaders with a sense of purpose feel better about their life direction. They align their goals with their personal values and find significance in their efforts. Leaders with purpose are optimistic and hopeful. They live and work with confidence and positivity instead of fears and insecurities. They perform better. They are satisfied with their jobs and commit to their organizations[3].

PURPOSE IN LEADER DEVELOPMENT: THE PURPOSE WEB OF BELIEF[SM]

The third web of belief for leader development is purpose. It encompasses a leader's passions, intentions, performance, and service to others. Purpose is the role one fills, the work one does, and the life one engages in. As we move through the stages of life, we use purpose to fulfill our basic human needs for food and shelter, safety and security, love and belonging, self-esteem, and self-actualization[4]. The Purpose Web of Belief is based in self-knowledge, decision-making, self-regulation, and courage. Living with purpose and meaning is imperative for leaders to be successful, help others achieve, and contribute to our organizations.

Leaders with purpose become dreamers and visionaries. We discover what is meaningful for our lives and careers. As we live and work with purpose, we use our natural talents and follow our passions. We establish a personal mission. We set and achieve goals aligned with our values. We engage with tenacity to achieve life and career milestones. We persist in the face of challenges and unenjoyable tasks. Purpose propels achievements which fit our beliefs and fulfill our dreams.

Purpose becomes the basis for a leader's motivation and resolve. It builds enthusiasm, dedication and perseverance. Leaders use the Purpose Web of Belief to understand and articulate the reasons, or the whys, for our actions. When circumstances change, or we experience setbacks, we remain flexible and adaptable. We set new goals and dream new dreams. We are free and capable to adjust our direction to better align with who we are and what we want to become. Remaining purposeful in the face of challenge and change builds our character[5].

Gaining competencies within the Purpose Web of Belief continues over a lifetime. By setting goals and attaching meaning to our actions, we use our talents, develop new skills, and assert our true selves. Leaders with purpose stay on course. We develop important self-leadership skills. We feel good about both what we have accomplished, and what we have not accomplished. We are hopeful about what can yet be achieved. We have the motivation to always keep trying or to start again[6].

REFLECTION ACTIVITY 5-1: THE PURPOSE WEB OF BELIEF IN YOUR LIFE

Using the definition of the Purpose Web of Belief, note ways you might be using it in your life or work.

Aspects of the Purpose Web of Belief	How do I practice this in life or work today?	How can I use or improve this in the future?
I believe in having a personal mission		
I know what I am passionate about		
I contribute to others in my work role		
I contribute to others through service		
I contribute to others in my personal role(s)		

UNDERSTANDING THE PURPOSE WEB OF BELIEF[SM]
PURPOSE IN LEADERSHIP TODAY

The meaning of life is to find your gift. The purpose of life is to give it away.

PABLO PICASSO[7]

Victor Frankl's book, *Man's Search for Meaning*[8], is a bestselling autobiography about how he used positivity to endure and survive in a concentration camp. Frankl believed humans have the will and the freedom to search for meaning in their lives. His work marked the emergence of positive psychology, a hallmark of 21st century leadership styles and theories[9]. He teaches us to make sense of life's negative experiences, to better cope with them, and to maintain overall well-being. Purpose motivates us to set meaningful goals, remain hopeful, and stay focused on results.

Purpose is visionary, motivational, and intentional

Setting one's purpose, and acting purposefully, is personal and unique. It determines where we direct our attention, who we spend time with, and what we do. It starts with self-knowledge of our natural capabilities, callings, and interests. We discover reasons for all we do. We make our whys our priorities[10]. We resolve to live out our passions and aspirations. To find purpose, we allow ourselves to dream. We reflect on what motivates us from within. We ruminate about what a meaningful life and career will look like. We identify what we care about and what we enjoy at each age and stage of life. We believe our efforts are important and will benefit others.

Purpose is about setting courageous goals

Goal setting was introduced into business in the mid-20th century. It remains a compelling process for motivating ourselves and others[11]. Purposeful leaders are not afraid to set lofty, or seemingly unrealistic, goals. We courageously navigate a path to these goals. We commit to challenging, but not impossible plans, then use energy, drive, and grit to stay on course. Following one's passions and living with purpose involves assertiveness and bravery.

Goals and plans based on visions and dreams are powerful. When focused on purpose, leaders work through bumps in the road, disappointments, mistakes, and failures. We find creative strategies to solve problems along the way. We use challenges to build stronger character and an array of coping skills. After reaching an objective, we become motivated to take next steps and learn new skills. Our purposeful experiences develop our confidence, intention, and resolve. Continuing to set and achieve challenging goals improves a leader's self-efficacy, or belief we can effectively perform a certain skill or task. Purpose drives our motivation to continue learning, leading, and achieving. We forge new solutions and paths for our career and life.

Purpose applies to our every action, every day

Using purpose, leaders set long term goals. We also know the reasons and intentions for our day-to-day activities and tasks. Committing to purpose means setting priorities, managing our time, and staying focused on performance in the present and for the future. Leaders with purpose use time management and planning tools. We improve our productivity and job satisfaction because every item on our to-do list ties back to a purpose and a plan.

Leadership Case: Jason and the Purpose Web of Belief

> Jason, a single parent of a toddler, was in an MBA evening program. During the day, he worked at a large chain store selling appliances. Jason always arrived early for class and commented about how much he disliked his job. He couldn't wait to finish his MBA to change employers and roles. I asked Jason why he held this job. He said it paid well enough to help him care for his young son, and the hours fit for his parenting role and his MBA courses. As a developing leader, Jason did have a purpose in his employment. This job enabled him to pursue his goal of getting a master's degree, and it paid the bills. In addition, working for a large company gave him perspective on how organizations work, an opportunity to network with managers, and information about what he would, and would not, like in a future employer. Using the Purpose Web of Belief, Jason put a different spin on his short-term work situation and continued his motivation to finish his MBA.
>
> *Which of your goals and plans involve doing something difficult or temporarily unpleasant?*

Purpose builds confidence, hope, and well-being
Only about half of us are naturally optimistic[12]. Life circumstances, or our collection of fears and doubts, may cause us to become negative or cynical. Yet, who wants to work for, or even with, someone who is pessimistic, complaining, or mean? To maintain forward energy and stick to a purpose, leaders need a positive mindset based in hope. They must exude optimism if they want to motivate others to get things done.

When the chips are down, leaders reflect about purpose. We remember our successes. We find reasons to continue working toward our goals. As we use purpose over time, we build confidence and self-esteem. We believe we can accomplish good things. We learn how to persist and persevere. We improve our capacities for taking initiative to solve complex problems. Believing in purpose generates more drive, energy, and competency to set the next goal. We improve our life satisfaction and our mental health[13]. When we make choices that naturally motivate us, we reach a state of eudemonia: a sense of happiness from doing good for ourselves and others. We live and work with confidence and hope.

Purpose changes and evolves
For some leaders, purpose stays the same over time. For others, purpose is organic. The best-laid plans are not always completed on their original timetable. Life happens; environments change. In our chaotic and uncertain world, no job or organization is guaranteed to stay the same, as new knowledge emerges and technology progresses. Workers at every level face changes in job descriptions, bosses, organizational structures, and processes. Leaders must adapt or change our purpose to address challenges, respond to threats, and pursue new opportunities. We learn new skills, discover new passions, and

take on new roles. We set fresh expectations for ourselves. We reset our paths. We continue to use our will and our freedom to find meaning in our life and work.

SELF ASSESSMENT 5-2: HOW YOU LIVE WITH PURPOSE

Think back over the last day or the last week. List three things you did, large or small. Fill in the chart with your purpose, or purposes, for your actions.

A task or activity I completed	My purpose(s) or reason(s) for this action

LEADER COMPETENCIES & STYLES WITHIN THE PURPOSE WEB OF BELIEF[SM]

Self-leadership, emotional intelligence, and authentic leadership competencies
Using purpose in leader development builds emotional intelligence capacities for self-awareness, motivation, and especially self-regulation. As they define their purposes, leaders become aware of what motivates them and what they can accomplish. They become self-propelled and self-controlled. Followers find them conscientious and trustworthy[14].

Competencies in self-awareness and self-direction set authentic leaders apart. The Purpose Web of Belief guides them to articulate their values and needs. As they understand the reasons for their decisions and actions, they become comfortable expressing their true beliefs to others. Authentic leaders use meaningful goals to live and work with passion and self-discipline[15]. They clearly communicate their purpose to motivate followers and become trusted role models.

Transformational leadership, crisis leadership, and change leadership competencies
To manage crisis, change, and transformation, leaders need decisiveness and persistence. Change leaders use purpose to set direction for themselves and their followers. They communicate a vision, create a sense of urgency, map a route, overcome roadblocks, and navigate detours. They track progress, then persevere and persist in the face of obstacles[16]. Crisis leaders with purpose mobilize collective action and set accountability for follow-through. Transformational leaders use visioning and goal setting for intellectual stimulation and inspirational motivation. They engage followers in positive and meaningful change, teaching them to live and work with purpose.

Strategic, complexity, adaptive, and executive leadership competencies
Adaptive leaders use goal setting to overcome difficulties related to chaos and uncertainty. They identify challenges and use purpose to motivate followers. Complexity leaders respond to emerging realities and systemic change with meaningful plans[17]. Executive leaders decide what needs to be done, set clear strategies, develop actions plans, take responsibility, and run productive meetings[18].

Servant leadership, connective leadership, and shared leadership competencies
Servant leaders and connective leaders are naturally inspired to help others find purpose because they focus on what is good for their followers. Leaders with these people-centered and collaborative styles facilitate shared decision-making to find common needs, then develop visions and goals to advance everyone's well-being[19]. They guide followers to find purpose and meaning in their life and work. Connective leaders and shared leaders serve the common good by engaging followers in coordinated action to reach their goals. They encourage others to be passionate about the work they do. They model the way, inspire shared vision, challenge the process, enable others to act, and encourage the heart, all with meaning and purpose[20].

HOW TO APPLY THE PURPOSE WEB OF BELIEF[SM] IN YOUR LEADER DEVELOPMENT

Dream and envision
Finding purpose starts with imagining and visioning. Take time to brainstorm about who you are, what you can become, and your wildest dreams. What if geography, or others' expectations, didn't matter? What would you do? Where would you live? What would your aspirations be? What would you be doing today if you could do, or be, anything you want, with no worries about finances or security? The answers to these questions are clues to understanding your passions. Use this input to articulate your dreams. Build an outline for a purpose-full life plan. Continue visioning about who you are and what you want to do. Think about how you will incorporate your dreams into your life and career.

REFLECTION EXERCISE 5-3: WHAT ARE YOU PASSIONATE ABOUT?

Fill in the chart about how you feel about what you do and have done.

	Things I enjoyed doing	Things I wish I had done
In the past week		
In the past month		
When I was 7 years old		
When I was 18		
When I was 25		

A. Are there times when you get into a flow and lose track of time? What are you doing during these times?

B. Review your chart. What are the themes? In other words: What do you love to do? What are your passions?

Identify what inspires you

Your beliefs and values guide your sense of right and wrong, drive your judgments, and set your standards of behavior. They direct your activities and the life decisions you make. Use the Purpose Web of Belief to define what is meaningful in your life. What is important to you? What is of worth to you? How do you spend your time and money? Who are your role models? Why? What values do they inspire in you?

Studies show we do not work for money. We work to assert our independence, define our identity, interact with others, and engage in meaningful activity[23]. Why do you work? Think about one or two of your major life decisions so far. Why did you make them? What inspired you? Why and how were you motivated to choose what you did? Can you find any common values you used for your choices? Reflect on what you value to make sense of the seemingly unrelated activities and pursuits in your life. Utilize purpose when you pursue new opportunities, discover new passions, or find new paths.

Use the exercise below to identify your top three to five core values. Do you see how your values convert to behaviors? When making decisions, even minor ones, use your core values as a mirror and a checkpoint. Make meaningful choices. Be sure your daily, weekly, and monthly activities reflect and support your core values. Are you living and leading with purpose?

REFLECTION EXERCISE 5-4: PINPOINT YOUR VALUES

Fill in the charts below to determine your top values.

Two major life decisions	1.	2.
What motivated me?		
Two daily or weekly activities	1.	2.
What motivated me?		

A. List five values you subscribe to. Writing each value on a card or sticky note is another way to do this. You can sort and re-sort the cards as you determine your priorities.

My values	How this value connects to my life decisions	How this value connects to my regular activities	Other notes about this value

B. Choose the two values that most often guide your decisions and actions, motivate you to do your best work, live your best life, and do good for yourself and others. Write a sentence or two with your own definitions and why they are your core values.

My top two values	My definition of this value	My reasons for this value

Write a personal mission statement

Most organizations post a mission statement on their website, in their marketing materials, or on their office walls. The mission guides the ethics, activities, and outcomes of the organization. Individual leaders also need a mission statement, stemming from your values and guiding your aspirations.

Discover and record your life reasons and meanings in a personal mission statement. Ask yourself: How am I unique compared to others in my life and work environment? What is my identity, drawn from my values, beliefs, and passions? What do I stand for? What am I here to do? Connect your mission to your goals and actions day-to-day and year-to-year. Use your mission statement to find a purpose for everything you do. Stay aware of how and why you are living and leading with meaning and purpose. Your mission statement guides your conscience and your pursuits. It helps you make sense of your life.

EXERCISE 5-5: WRITING A PERSONAL MISSION STATEMENT

Review exercises 5-3 and 5-4 about your values and passions. Answer these questions: What do I live for? What/who creates meaning for me in life? Do I answer to a higher power? What are my reasons for doing what I do every day? Is there a reason or purpose for my life that is larger than just me? Combine these answers into a personal mission statement. You may begin with a draft, then revise it later.

Example of A Personal Mission Statement

I strive . . .
To be open minded and willing to accept situations I neither choose nor understand.
To continue to grow emotionally, intellectually, and creatively.
To bring a calming effect to the people whose lives I touch.
To base my life decisions on both common sense and heart-felt emotion.
To be loved by those closest to me for patience and unselfishness.

Be hopeful

Real life is fraught with challenges and crucibles. Moods and negative emotions creep in. The good news for leaders is optimism can be learned. To become more optimistic, keenly engage your powers to think about your own thinking. Stop yourself when your thoughts or actions head in a negative direction. Use practical optimism to remain positive overall yet understand and accept negative events and times. When you fail or encounter difficulties, gather hope. Use self-talk statements on a bad day or during tough circumstances. Tell yourself: *This too will pass. I've been through other tough times, and I got through. After a good night's sleep, or a good meal, I will feel better.* Notice what a difference a day, week, or year makes by looking back to see how your past problems resolved or dissolved over time. Ask yourself what you are learning, or what you are supposed to learn, during difficult times. Note what you learned and apply it to the future.

Focus on what is good about you and what you do well. Write a short list of the accomplishments in your life so far and the good things you do daily or weekly. Add notes about compliments or encouragement you get from others.

Review your lists. This is proof you have made positive progress in your life and career. Give thanks for these good things and accomplishments in your life and work every day. Slowly but surely, you will increase self-esteem and positive beliefs about yourself. You will understand what works for you, how you get things done, and how others respond to you. Use this confidence to persevere and persist.

Train yourself to reverse pessimistic reactions. When you want to think or say something negative, wait 24 seconds before responding. Next, train yourself to wait 24 minutes, and then 24 hours before reacting negatively to what you hear or see. Your reactions will become more objective and positive with the passage of time[24]. When you seem to be on the wrong track or losing hope, practice thankfulness and gratitude to rewire your brain toward resilience and hope. Think about the people and places in your life. Do they help or hurt your state of mind? Surround yourself with positive, can-do people. Be inspired by others' optimism and success. Post quotations, happy photos, and inspirational pictures on your walls and mobile devices.

One of the most powerful abilities of human nature is our potential to take on new challenges, persevere through them, and learn from them. Take on challenges and expect good outcomes with a growth mindset. Believe you can overcome obstacles, finish a task, or achieve something by expending more effort and more creativity. Leaders with a growth mindset know if they simply try harder, good things will happen. Let mistakes and setbacks become motivational. Find the positives in your negatives. You will develop coping skills and a propensity for hope and practical optimism. Use your strengths to help you, and the people around you, to flourish[25].

REFLECTION 5-6: OPTIMISM IN YOUR LIFE

Fill in the blanks about your optimism and growth mindset.

Am I naturally optimistic or pessimistic? How do I know this?
How/when can I use the Rule of 24 to think and react more positively?
What am I thankful for?
When I become negative, or start to doubt my abilities or purpose, what can I say to myself to return to a positive mindset? Write an uplifting statement you can memorize and use:

Find our flow and build momentum.
Intrinsic motivation arises within when you pursue something naturally interesting and engaging. This form of motivation generates direction and persistence. Becoming intrinsically motivated produces an energized state within your leadership. You gain self-esteem and work toward self-actualization. To increase intrinsic motivation, remember what you are passionate about. Do something related to your passions at least once a week. Try to align career and life choices with what motivates you, gives you energy, and puts you in flow for the long term. If your motivation is self-determined, or driven from within, you experience enjoyment and vitality in life and career[26].

We all have times and situations when we are engaged and immersed in an activity, and we lose track of time. We are content, motivated, and want to continue the endeavor indefinitely. This is called being in flow[27]. To discover what puts you in a state of flow, think about your younger self. What did you enjoy doing then? What motivated you and made you happy? In your current stage of your life, when are you content? When are you motivated? What activities increase your energy level? What are you doing when your motivation and energy are depleted? What makes you tired or grumpy? Are you following your own dreams, or are you in a job, profession, or lifestyle that others have convinced you to follow? When are you most motivated to set a goal or accomplish something? What makes you feel alive? What makes you joyful? What fulfills you[28]?

Once you find your flow and become internally motivated, reaching one goal leads to setting another. We build positive resolve to go on to the next goal. Confidence builds. We gain courage. We believe we can accomplish more by continuing to try. We assume all will be done, and all will be good. Our achievements spiral forward and up. This is positive momentum!

Be a planner: Set intentions and goals
Try to align career and life choices with what motivates you, gives you energy, and puts you in flow for the long term. Believe your energy is unlimited and your wildest dreams can come true. The Buddhist tradition encourages us to follow our imagination and align our inner desires with the power of intention. When we add our thoughts and feelings to nurture our imagination and internal motivation, we manifest our desired results. To put the power of intention into play, be creative, kind, loving, expansive, abundant, and receptive[29].

As a leader who believes in purpose, set goals for your life and work. Write a two-year plan for yourself. Make it challenging, but doable. Include specifics for the first year, with action items and concrete tasks. As you complete your objectives (or not), note what was done and how you thought and felt about what you did. During the second year of the plan, review it. Write another two-year plan, adjusted to what you have completed. Incorporate new opportunities, newly discovered passions, and your current dreams. On a day-to-day and month-to-month basis, this is your blueprint for meaning, purpose, and motivation to lead yourself and others.

Develop purposeful habits: Make it happen
Once you are a goal-setter, you also need to become a pacesetter. Planning involves the right brain for creativity and vision. Following through requires

left brain skills: concrete thinking and self-regulation. Schedule your dreams into your life. Use self-discipline, self-determination, attention to detail, procedural skills, and time management to stay on track. Break down general goals into small steps and quick tasks that are easily completed. Use a planner. Set daily, weekly, and monthly priorities. As you write a task on your planner or to-do list, also note an estimate of the amount of time it will take. Then record the actual time the task took. This will help you schedule the time needed for similar initiatives in the future.

Every month or two, review what you have done. Determine how you used your time and resources to complete your plans (or not). Learn what is reasonable to accomplish and how long it takes to make progress toward your goals. If an action or project was not on your list of goals, ask yourself how it aligns (or not) with your overall purpose. Should it be included? Is it a sign of a new opportunity or a change in direction? Edit your action plans accordingly. Adjust your expectations, and know what you can get done when, where, and how. Continue this micro-level action planning. Always have meaningful to-dos on your calendar. *Chapter 8 of this book provides detailed instructions for developing a creative and purposeful plan for your leadership and your life.*

Celebrate your accomplishments

To understand what you can yet achieve, it is important to look back, not just to move forward. At least monthly, reflect on your accomplishments, no matter how small. Pinpoint the competencies you used, what you learned, and the capacities you expanded. Congratulate and reward yourself for following your plan. Believe in who you are, what you did, and what you can do. Know that you are following your passions, using your talents, and getting things done. Recognize and acknowledge the good within you. Believe in yourself and enjoy your purpose-full life. Gather up energy, confidence and momentum to stay on course and set next-level goals.

Change direction as needed

As the proverb states, *the best laid plans of mice and men oft go awry*. With the demands of 21st century life and work, we might even say our plans always go awry. Goal setting and goal-accomplishing are never perfect. Life happens, and we stray from our intentions. Other needs or circumstances derail our progress. As leaders and adults, our interests and passions change. Our competencies expand. Our possibilities and opportunities open wider and further.

It is okay and even necessary to readjust or refresh your vision, mission, goals, or timetables. Remember, your purpose is organic. Rewriting your plans and committing to revised goals builds higher-level skills in decision-making, self-motivation, self-regulation, and self-leadership. You become more creative in problem-solving, action-planning, and implementation. You live with more passion and fulfill more needs. You become satisfied and self-actualized in your life and work.

Leadership Case: Changing Purpose through Life

Many of us spend our first half of life learning a set of career skills, establishing our lifestyle, and creating our village of family and friends. At the same time, we may be raising a family and providing service to our community. The first few decades of life are energetic, intense, and achievement-oriented. By our 4th or 5th decade, we may have many achievements, and sometimes we have done too much. For some, the body responds by getting sick; for others, the mind and spirit become bored or discontent. We may experience life changes due to failed relationships, losses, broken promises, or unmet goals. We can become frustrated and confused about our purpose in life and career. Uncertainty sets in. We may start to wonder: What is next for me? How will I continue to be fulfilled and satisfied? We begin to seek something more.

These feelings of futility and lack of meaning in life can return in the 6th or 7th decades of life, when our careers end and our bodies show signs of age and wear. Do we wind down and give up? Or are these the times to find new purpose and set new goals? Excellent books and podcasts are available to understand and overcome these dilemmas. Some are listed in the Additional Resources section of this chapter.

Those who believe in purpose finish strong. We muster up tenacity to discover new passions and opportunities. The possibilities are endless if only we take the time to discover them and resolve to commit anew. As we navigate our second half of life, we can create exciting next stage plans. Using purpose and practical optimism, we grow as leaders, family members, and friends. We sail toward our sunsets wiser, happier, and more productive than ever.

When in your life or career have you changed your purpose? What happened next? What did you learn about yourself during that time?

ASSESSMENT EXERCISE 5-7: PURPOSE SKILLS & MINDSETS

Record your thoughts about how to use these tools for purpose in your leadership. You may have more than one idea for an item. You may have no comments or ideas for others.

Purpose Skills and Mindsets	How I Can Use This to Improve my Purpose and Leadership
Dreaming and envisioning	
Identifying core values and inspiration	
Living according to a mission statement	
Being hopeful	
Finding flow and building momentum	
Planning with intention and goals	
Developing purposeful habits	
Changing direction as needed	

BEYOND THE INDIVIDUAL: THE PURPOSE WEB OF BELIEF[SM] IN TEAMS & ORGANIZATIONS

Leaders using the Purpose Web of Belief influence followers toward meaningful behavior and meaningful contributions. Purposeful organizations connect performance and profit with positive outcomes for employees, stakeholders, and society. They set norms for working together productively. They inspire individuals to come together and be part of something bigger than themselves[30].

An organization's purpose is articulated via vision, mission, and values, then translated into strategic plans. These direct decisions, actions, and practices across the organization and provide stability in times of uncertainty. The planning process creates sense, meaning, and motivation for all. Detailed implementation plans with measurable goals guide groups and individuals. Team members understand how their roles and projects connect to the organization's values and purpose[31].

With organizational plans and values as their beacon, leaders instill a sense of purpose in their followers. They draw a clear map for individuals and teams to interact, share intentions, and collaborate[32]. Running productive meetings is an aspect of leading with purpose and facilitates the successful achievement of team goals. Meeting agendas are another way to assure all activities have a purpose, a timeline, and connect to goals.

Believing in a shared purpose drives individuals and teams to be courageous and confident. Teams who agree on goals, roles, and norms make better decisions. They align, cooperate, and manage conflict as they solve complex problems. They assume responsibility and contribute to the organization's mission. When employees understand the organization's purpose, they increase their engagement in their work and commitment to the organization. They challenge themselves and others to expend more effort when faced with uncertainty or complexity. They set and reach stretch goals. They cooperate with change initiatives. They remain ethical in their activities and their results because they are doing good for themselves and their organization. This contributes to job satisfaction, employee retention, and employee well-being[33].

THE PURPOSE WEB OF BELIEF[SM] IN ACTION

Ellen Johnson Sirleaf: African Stateswoman, Freedom Fighter, Prisoner, Nobel Peace Laureate[34]

The future belongs to us, because we have taken charge of it. We have the commitment, we have the resourcefulness, and we have the strength of our people to share the dream across Africa of clean water for all.

ELLEN JOHNSON SIRLEAF

Ellen Johnson Sirleaf left Liberia to get her college education in the U.S.

With a masters degree from Harvard, she returned to her native country determined to reform the corrupt government there and establish freedoms for all. While serving as finance minister in the 1980's, she was imprisoned ten years for criticizing the government, and then exiled for 12 more years. Two prison terms did not deter her. She returned to Liberia to champion her values of integrity and equality. Sirleaf was elected the first woman President of an African country in 2006, with resolve to build hope and improve the wellbeing for the people of Liberia. Her courageous initiatives over the decade reduced corruption and established general equality in the government. She was awarded a Nobel Peace Prize in 2011 for her efforts to further women's rights. Thanks to her resolve and persistent follow-through, Liberia's economy expanded. With a seemingly unachievable vision and lofty goals, she broke barriers. Liberia has enjoyed two decades of peace and economic stability. It boasts the highest freedom scale rating of all the emerging democracies in Africa. The country has made much progress establishing order and providing civil liberties to citizens.

Jeff Bezos: Technology Entrepreneur, Business Mogul, Inventor[35]

Where you are going to spend your time and your energy is one of the most important decisions you get to make in life.
JEFF BEZOS

Jeffrey Preston Bezos showed he could set and reach stretch goals when he established an institute for youth creativity while still in high school. With a computer science and engineering education at the dawn of the internet age, he resolved to create electronic businesses, starting first with books, then establishing the largest virtual retailer and cloud computing service on the globe. Bezos energetically builds first-of-their-kind businesses. His life purpose is to invent leading-edge enterprises, but not with the intention of becoming wealthy. As a testament to his drive and motivation, his business accomplishments and his accumulation of wealth are always described with superlatives. Regardless of the complexities and challenges entwined in dangerous work environments and labor shortages, he expects Amazon to be Earth's Best Employer and the Earth's Safest Place to Work. Bezos focuses on productivity and efficiency. His *two pizzas rule* for meetings limits attendees so they can get to work and get things done. He is an inventor and entrepreneur. He believes purpose, enthusiasm, and passion for what you do generates job satisfaction. When he began Blue Origin, he was clear and assured of his why: to build an infrastructure for communities in space where people live and work peacefully to benefit the earth. His motto for this space travel company is *step by step, ferociously.*

Malala Yousafzai: Social Activist, Global Spokesperson, Nobel Laureate[36]

Malala Yousafzai's father motivated her to help women and girls in Pakistan get an education. At age 11, she became a blogger and international television personality who publicly defied her government's ban on women's schooling.

Her intention to change the social system became more fervent at age 15 when she survived an assassination attempt by the Taliban. She developed as a globally renowned speaker, championing education and social justice for women across the globe. She speaks with courage, passion, and inspiration to expose the dilemma of girls and women denied education in many countries. Malala was awarded the Nobel Peace Prize at age 17 for her purposeful work.

Howard Schulz: Business CEO, Author, Sports Team Owner[37]

You must find something that you deeply love and are passionate about and are willing to sacrifice a lot to achieve.
HOWARD SCHULTZ

Howard D. Schultz envisioned a coffee house space between home and work where people could converse, connect, and build community. He established the first Starbucks store in 1971 and motivated his employees, from executives to baristas, to fashion a compassionate company and celebrate success. He drove his employees to achieve his purpose by offering health care coverage for both full and part-time people and encouraging them to become equity partners by investing in Starbucks stock. During his tenure, he built a $30 billion worldwide company, with the same atmosphere and feel in every location. Schultz retired after 14 years as CEO, but the company lost its way and veered from its original purpose. He returned as CEO for 9 more years to rebuild momentum, then retired again. Five years later, he unretired once again to mentor a successor who would keep the company on track with his original intentions. He did everything in his power to keep the company true to his vision. Schultz's commitment to build his dream and achieve his company's purpose seems unending.

Simon Sinek: Author, Consultant, Teacher[38]

People don't buy what you do; they buy why you do it.
SIMON SINEK

As a marketing executive, Simon Oliver Sinek became melancholy and discontented. He realized he knew what he did and how, but he didn't know why he was doing what he was doing. He established The Optimism Company to encourage leaders to build hope and positivity for themselves and their employees. His question to all became: What is your why? His simple and direct communications style inspires and challenges people to articulate their reasons for what they are doing and where they are going in life and career. He teaches performance management and communication to help people become satisfied and in flow with themselves and their work. Sinek believes if a company has purpose in its culture, employees will engage. He encourages us to set courageous goals and become comfortable with the uncomfortable. Sinek wants us to keep the effort going when we are stuck or puzzled by a problem or situation, and just figure it out.

CONCLUSION

Believing in purpose drives us to clarify our capabilities and drive toward achievement. The Purpose Web of Belief guides leaders to dream and vision, set goals, and manage time. When we connect our purpose and plans to our passions, interests, and values, we align our goals with what we love and what we believe. We discover the whys for our accomplishments. A sense of purpose helps us find meaning and motivation for life and career. Designing a roadmap for reaching our goals makes us certain about who we are and where we are going. We use purpose to adapt to threats and seize opportunities. Once we get to the destination, we celebrate. We become motivated to start the next phase of our journey. We build self-confidence. A leader's purpose may change and evolve over time. Finding new purpose and setting new goals is courageous and necessary. The Purpose Web of Belief builds next level leadership skills for strategic thinking, decision-making, self-leadership, and self-esteem. Individuals with purpose are healthier and happier in their jobs and in their life.

ADDITIONAL RESOURCES

A New Earth: Awakening to Your Life's Purpose. Eckhart Tolle. Plume, 2005
Do It! Let's Get Off Our Buts. Peter McWilliams. Prelude Press, 1994
Finding Flow. Mihaly Csikszentmihalyi. Basic Books, 1997
Finding Your Strength in Difficult Times: A Book of Meditations. David Viscott. Contemporary Books, 1993
Grit: The Power of Passion and Perseverance. Angela Duckworth, Scribner, 2016 Growth Mindset. Carol Dweck, Ph.D.
Half-Time: Changing Your Game Plan from Success to Significance. Bob Buford. Zondervan, 1994
Listening to Midlife. Mark Gerzon, Shambhala, 1996
My Time; Making the Most of the Rest of Your Life. Abigail Trafford. Baic Books, 2004
Synchro Destiny. Deepak Chopra. Ebury Publishing, 2003.
The Effective Executive: The Definitive Guide to Getting the Right Things Done. Peter F. Drucker. Harper, 2006
You Can't Afford the Luxury of a Negative Thought. Peter McWilliams. Prelude Press, 1995
The Next Level: Breakthrough Performance Anchored by Faith. Michelle Gethers-Clark. WestBow Press, 2012
The 7 Habits of Highly Effective People. Stephen R. Covey. Free Press, 2004
Wishes Fulfilled. Dr. Wayne W. Dyer. Hay House, 2012

CHAPTER APPENDIX

The PURPOSE Web of Belief[SM]	Competencies & Mindsets Developed Within Leadership Theories and Styles
Complexity/Strategic/ Adaptive/Crisis/Executive Leadership Capacities	High performance, producer, director, monitor, vision, emphasize mutual goals for correlation, foster emergent structure, administrative leadership, bring best of self to organization, explore solutions, identify challenges, focus on difficulties, streamline decision making, prepared, resilient, convert knowledge into action, develop action plans, take responsibility for decisions and communications[39], focus on opportunities, run productive meetings, production for the organization, actively engage[40]
Shared/Connective/ Servant/ Team/Leadership and Followership Capacities	Goal orientation for self and others, coordination, action mindset, choice/commitment, inspirational, visionary, concern for production, incentive for performance, collective achievement[41], sustainability mindset, model the way, inspire a shared vision, enable others to act[42], team self-observation, team goal-setting, team cue modification, team self-reward, team self-talk, team mental imagery, set goals, decision-making, planning, implementation, evaluation, structure[43], follower performance, engagement[44], persuasion, conceptualization, foresight[45]
Authentic Leadership/ Self Leadership/Emotional Intelligence Capacities	Self-regulation, goals, motives for self-improvement, self-determination, purpose, self-discipline, master own tasks, intrinsic/excels, competitive/outperforms, power/takes charge[46] map the route, navigate detours and roadblocks, natural rewards, constructive mindsets, set standards, self-management, positive psychology, self-reward; search for purpose, be specific, set short- and long-term goals, increase positive cues, reduce negative cues, have purpose in life, focus on natural rewards, self-talk[47], passion, consistency[48], courage, good decision making, motivation[49]
Change Leadership & Transformational Leadership Capacities	Communicate clear vision, persevere and persist[50], sense of urgency, vision, communicate the vision, create short term wins, continuous improvement, keep gaining, anchor change in the culture, institutionalize change, inspire people to act, build momentum, pursue a compelling and clear vision of the future, guide, coordinate, enable action by removing barriers, work nimbly, generate impact quickly, recognize wins, sustain acceleration[51], inspirational motivation[52]

**To be yourself
in a world that is constantly trying
to make you something else
is the greatest accomplishment.**

RALPH WALDO EMERSON

CHAPTER 6

THE AUTHENTICITY WEB OF BELIEF^{SM}

> Belief in continuous discovery and understanding of one's identity and one's convictions, accompanied by clear expression and acknowledgement of the genuine self in interpersonal communications and behaviors.

WHAT IS AUTHENTICITY IN THE 21ST CENTURY?

A way of being and thinking
Authenticity was introduced by the philosopher Sartre less than 100 years ago. He believed humans are responsible for creating values and meaning in their lives. He wrote: "Man first exists, then encounters the world...and continues defining himself as long as he is in this world[1]." Today psychologists identify authenticity as part of social cognition, or our understanding of ourselves in relation to the people and places in our life. Becoming authentic involves freeing ourselves to determine our beliefs and behave genuinely. We use self-awareness to understand who we are, what we believe and think, and how we present ourselves in our world. Authenticity is now associated with positive psychology and the related characteristics of efficacy, optimism, hope, and resilience[2].

Understanding and acting on morals and convictions
Authentic behavior is connected to moral reasoning and moral development. It becomes the outward expression of deep and lasting commitment to one's identity and values. Living authentically means always acting on principles. Authentic leaders ascribe to a clear set of internal moral standards and use them to guide their decisions and behaviors. They remain loyal to a code of conduct and have reasons for their choices every day. Followers want to interact with, and learn from, people who know who they are and readily express their convictions. People who are authentic in today's world gain credibility and the trust of others[3].

Admitting the bounds and limits of the genuine self
Authentic individuals know who they are and where they have come from. They discover their strengths and weaknesses, then showcase their positives. They understand what they are capable of and what they are not capable of. Most importantly, they admit their shortcomings to others, listen to advice, and accept criticism. Authentic leaders learn and change by analyzing their mistakes and failures. They learn to communicate assertively. They genuinely express and confidently articulate what they believe. To others, they seem humble, yet smart.

AUTHENTICITY IN LEADER DEVELOPMENT: THE AUTHENTICITY WEB OF BELIEF[SM]

Authenticity in leadership is based in conviction, values, and identity. It is marked by behaviors genuine and original to an individual's self-concept. The Authenticity Web of Belief encourages us to excavate our true self by studying our own stories. We commit to uncovering how we came to be who we are. We reconstruct our past and present experiences to discern their effects on our beliefs, motivation, and interpersonal interactions[4]. We continuously explore our core values, beliefs, and capabilities. Our findings help us develop and use our unique talents, and act on our moral convictions. We make sense of ourselves and our life. As our authentic self grows over the career and the lifetime, we learn to navigate more complex situations and challenges[5].

Leaders practicing authenticity gain confidence in our own beliefs and competencies. We expand self-awareness and self-leadership, along with cognitive, emotional, and moral capacities. We develop high-level communication skills for sharing information and influencing others[6]. We learn to clearly articulate our beliefs, first internally, and then outwardly. Because authenticity is highly valued by younger generations, authentic leaders and followers become trusted role models, teachers, and agents of change. We encourage relationship-building for mutual benefit through genuine dialogue. Both leaders and followers who are authentic experience personal growth, improve communication skills, and build unencumbered relationships. Authentic leaders generate optimism for ourselves and hope for others[7].

Leaders' stories unfold through their lifetimes. We continue to be sculpted by new experiences. Using the Authenticity Web of Belief means always taking the time to be aware and understand how new events and encounters are contributing to the evolving self[8]. Educational experiences, people, crucibles, accomplishments, and life events shape our identity and moral compass. We discover new realities, gain new knowledge, and reach new conclusions. The positive evolution of self is fueled by self-reflection and self-leadership for the entire lifetime.

REFLECTION ACTIVITY 6-1: THE AUTHENTICITY WEB OF BELIEF IN YOUR LIFE

Using the definition of the Authenticity Web of Belief, note where and how you are using it.

Aspects of the Authenticity Web of Belief	How I practice this *at work*	How I practice this *at home*	How I practice this *with friends*	How I can use or improve this in the future
I continuously discover my identity and convictions				
I express and communicate my genuine self				

UNDERSTANDING THE AUTHENTICITY WEB OF BELIEF[SM]: AUTHENTICITY IN LEADERSHIP TODAY

Authentic leadership theory emerged in the 1990's from humanistic philosophy, with the underlying tenet that leaders can develop optimal self-esteem[9]. The leadership literature highlights authenticity as an intrapersonal, interpersonal, and organizational phenomenon. Experts believe leaders using an authentic style become increasingly self-actualized over their career and life spans[10].

To further understand authentic leadership, picture leaders from the past who positively impacted society: Martin Luther King, Jr., Ruth Bader Ginsburg, and Nelson Mandela. These individuals knew who they were and what they wanted to accomplish. They remained ever true to strong internal beliefs and standards. Also consider the authentic individuals who influence your own life—parents, grandparents, mentors, best friends, siblings, coworkers. These significant people in our lives readily and openly share their convictions and give us candid feedback. They treat us with tough love because they care about us and want us to become our best selves. Their words of wisdom resound in our heads throughout our lifetime. We remember their advice as we encounter challenges or make decisions.

REFLECTION ACTIVITY 6-2: WHO ARE YOUR AUTHENTIC LEADERS?

List two to three people you consider authentic leaders.

Figures from History or Current Events			
People in Your Life Today or In the Past			

Authenticity starts with self-discovery

Each of us is a unique biological genome, with a personal collection of DNA and experiences shared by no one else. The road to authenticity begins with deep understanding of who we are, what we believe, and what we can and cannot do. We must spend time and effort carefully reflecting on our thoughts and behaviors in various contexts over time[11]. We must go deep within to uncover the truths about our talents, our experiences, our hopes, and our fears. We use self-leadership to become clear about our strengths and shortcomings. We learn what, how, and why we do what we do and think what we think. As we develop and understand our authentic self, we use balanced processing of our thoughts, emotions, and behaviors to learn and grow from our experiences. As we gain self-understanding and confidence, we strengthen interpersonal relationships. We get things done, and we become believers in our ability to do more.

Using the Johari Window[12] is a simple way to view and understand our full and true self. Imagine your entire being, with all your skills, thoughts, emotions, and behaviors, as a window. In this window is the full repertoire of what we know and do not know about ourselves, as well as what others know and perceive about us. The Johari studies found individuals are aware of only and perceive about us. The Johari studies found individuals are aware of only a portion of their true self (the known) and show an even smaller portion of that self to others (the open area). Others who interact with us see differences from our own perceptions (the blind section). A large pane of the window is yet to be discovered (the unknown). The journey to authenticity involves careful review of our entire Johari window. Through self-observation, eliciting feedback from others, and regular reflection on all the panes of the window, we continuously discover more about our authentic self.

SELF-ASSESSMENT 6-3: YOUR JOHARI WINDOWPANES

Fill in a few things in each pane of the window: Your known, open and blind sections. In the unknown section, you might write a question or two you have about yourself.

My Johari Window Today

Unknown to Myself and Others		
Known Only to Myself	Open/ Shown to Others	Blind Spots/ Known by Others

Authenticity draws from the insights and answers in our stories

How do we learn who we really are? The data for analysis and reflection is buried in our life stories. Our answers emerge from the chronicles of our experiences, starting with our earliest memories. Putting together a lifeline of these stories, then reflecting on their meaning, creates the backdrop for understanding our mindsets and our aspirations. We uncover how our sagas molded our beliefs, behaviors, skills, and passions.

As part of our story, we go through life crucibles: significant events that shape our conscious and unconscious thinking, feeling, and actions[13]. Crucibles can be high points or low points in our life. To begin the journey to authenticity, we review details of the where, who, what, and how of these events. Why were they significant? Who did we share them with? What did they teach us? How are they still affecting our thoughts, decisions, and actions today? How we recovered from difficult times sheds light on our emotional strengths and coping skills. Often, our greatest challenges have the most impact on our life choices, long-term behaviors, lasting joys, and underlying fears.

Authenticity grounds our identity and frames our moral compass

Over the course of our lifetime, we move through stages of moral development and reasoning. As young children, we respond to right and wrong based on the need for obedience and the fear of punishment. During adolescence, we learn the conventions and laws of our social environment. As we move into adulthood, we explore variations to conventional law. We adjust our beliefs using our own logical conclusions. We better understand our choices and decisions. Some values and traditions become stronger, and more important, motivators. Our unique set of ethics and moral perspectives evolves[14]. These internal standards, our intuition, and our conscience become our guide. The essence of authenticity comes when our actions match our convictions and values.

Authenticity is based in a strong sense of personal identity. Understanding and accepting our unique identity, without judgment, makes us comfortable in our own skin. We become our own person, driven by qualities of the heart like passion, compassion, determination, and mental toughness. As we become more authentic, we build characteristics to better express our identity, such as courage and emotional intelligence[15]. Our individual character separates us from the rest of the pack.

Authenticity builds communications skills
Once we understand our identity, our capabilities, and our convictions, we need to go a step further. The evidence of authenticity is our ability to express and project the true self in interpersonal relationships and problem-solving. Authenticity becomes assertive when we articulate and act out our truths. We find our voice within our self, then speak out to others. As we increase our authenticity, we develop advanced communications skills to share core feelings, motives, and reasons for what we think and how we act. Authentic leaders easily engage in dialogue to manage conflict, negotiate shared understanding, and help colleagues avoid or resolve interpersonal differences. The Authenticity Web of Belief provides the basis for honest and open information-sharing between leaders and followers[16].

Authenticity builds confidence, self-esteem, and optimism
The more we know and accept about our authentic self, the more relaxed we become. We build positive psychological capital, or optimistic belief in our own capabilities. We are free to develop our strengths and explain our weaknesses. We become comfortable using our natural talents and following our passions. We radiate self-esteem when we walk into a room or begin to speak. Our body language and presence emanate not only truth and confidence, but also genuineness and humility. We become resilient in our responses to setbacks and challenges.

A powerful way to lead ourselves and others
Authenticity today is one of the most powerful leadership styles and the new charisma. Leaders practicing authenticity will deeply influence followers in the 21st century. Why? Because there is so much we need and want to do today. In our busy and chaotic existence, we appreciate genuine and transparent people to work for, work with, and learn from. Emerging leaders from the millennial and Z generations insist on authenticity and rate it amongst their highest values. They seek out authentic leaders[17].

Authentic leaders are true to self and build credibility with others. Leaders who operate authentically today are well-respected, even loved, by others. We do not put on airs or expect others to. These qualities are refreshing and motivating for followers. Followers listen to, and give their all in response to, what an authentic leader asks them to do.

SELF ASSESSMENT 6-4: YOUR PERSONALITY TRAITS

Write a few notes about your personality and the Big Five personality traits[18]

Personality Trait	How/when this shows (or not) in my personality	How this helps or hinders my life and leadership
Conscientiousness focus, direction, thoughtfulness		
Neuroticism moodiness, emotional instability		
Extroversion sociability, assertiveness		
Agreeableness trust, kindness, compassion		
Openness to Experience curiosity, imagination		

LEADER COMPETENCIES & STYLES IN THE AUTHENTICITY WEB OF BELIEF℠

Self-leadership and emotional intelligence competencies

The Authenticity Web of Belief is grounded in self-understanding, emotional awareness, and development of an accurate self-image. By naming, shaping, and celebrating their identity, leaders become independent and autonomous. They understand their roles and develop their own unique leadership style. They increase metacognitive skills (i.e. thinking about their own thinking) to become certain of their values and consistent in their communications and behaviors. Their self-image becomes accurate. They admit to, and learn from, their mistakes. They gain advanced capacity for the emotional intelligence characteristics of self-awareness and self-regulation. By communicating transparently and engaging in honest dialogue, authentic leaders build relational and social intelligence skills. They work through inner obstacles and take initiative to become self-motivated and self-controlled. They understand leader development as a lifelong process in which they are responsible for their own choices[19].

Ethical leadership competencies

The Authenticity Web of Belief is intertwined with ethical leadership. Authentic leaders model a positive moral identity based in a set of personal convictions.

Their values benefit both themselves and others. They use positive moral perspective and principled self-regulation to become honest colleagues and balanced decision-makers. They lead confidently and gain followers' trust[20].

Transformational leadership, adaptive leadership, complexity leadership, and change leadership competencies

In the face of complexity and crisis, transformational and change leaders courageously use their personal power to challenge processes and take calculated risks. They take initiative to actively engage others and contribute to needed change. They use their strengths to innovate, broker, and build coalitions as they adapt to new realities. Because of their credibility with peers and followers, authentic leaders transform people and organizations[21].

When leading change or complexity, authentic leaders are transparent about issues, needs, and resources. They use advanced communications and interpersonal skills to articulate ideas, generate dialogues, manage conflict, negotiate shared understanding, and manage change initiatives. In the face of crisis, their moral convictions and positive approaches help uplift others. As adaptive leaders, they influence and develop others to work though complex conditions and challenges[22].

Connective leadership, servant leadership, team leadership, and followership competencies

Authentic leaders develop connective and servant leadership competencies because they genuinely desire to serve others. They are more interested in empowering followers to make a difference than gaining power, money, or prestige for themselves[23]. The Authenticity Web of Belief develops humble leaders guided by passion and compassion. Authentic leaders recognize, use, and celebrate others' strengths and capabilities. They make everyone a hero. They utilize transparency and openness in teams and team leadership. They are competent facilitators, influencers, and commitment builders.

Followers with authenticity know themselves and understand their own talents and capabilities. They develop emotional intelligence capacities for self-awareness, self-discipline, motivation, empathy, and social skills[24]. They gain mindsets for patterning attention and strategic perspective-taking. They make sense of their own life stories and continue to grow as adults and as leaders. They accept, and learn from, feedback.

REFLECTION 6-5: AUTHENTIC LEADERSHIP AND YOU

Think of a current challenge in an interpersonal relationship at work or at home. How can you use authenticity to improve or solve this situation?

HOW TO APPLY THE AUTHENTICITY WEB OF BELIEF^{SM} IN YOUR LEADER DEVELOPMENT

Excavate your truths from your life stories
The first steps in authenticity involve becoming aware of who you are, what you believe, and what you can, and cannot, do. We excavate the stuff of our true selves by going back in time. As you think about your younger self, ask questions like: Who were you when you were 7, 12, 18, and 25 years old? What did you enjoy doing? Did you have any passions? How did you think? What values and beliefs did you have at that time? Who taught you and guided you? Who in your life influenced or inspired you, both positively and negatively? The answers to these questions are clues about how and why you became the person you are today[25].

Begin documenting your life story with a simple chart or life map. Use the life map exercise below to chart eight to ten significant events in your life. Include successes and high points, as well as failures and low points. Simply note what comes to mind. Pay special attention to the trials and negative events. Often, achievements such as a graduation, or obstacles such as the loss of a loved one, become crucibles, or significant, life-changing markers for our physical, mental, and spiritual growth. How you cope with crucibles, and what you learn from them, is key to understanding your competencies and your potential for growth.

Once you understand your own narrative, share it with others. Telling stories about your history at appropriate times and places helps others understand and accept you. Others come to know you as a real human with history and depth. Those around you learn from what you share. You build credible and meaningful relationships.

Life-mapping is an exercise you can repeat throughout your life. Each time you re-think and re-tell your story, you gain new insights about how you were shaped by your life events. You build more understanding and confidence to help with everyday challenges. You navigate better through new significant events and life phases. Continue to compose and tell your evolving story. There is always more to excavate from, and learn about, your authentic self.

Leadership Case: A Letter to Myself at High School Graduation

40 years after high school graduation, I found an 8-page letter to myself in a box of memorabilia. I did not remember writing it, but it truly reflected my core values and my personality. I had lost sight of some things that fed my spirit and other things that held me back. This letter was an amazing artifact as I worked to discover my authentic self. Today, I include stationery and an envelope in every high school graduation card I send. In the card, I tell the story of my letter to myself and encourage the graduate to write a letter to themself as well. Reviewing and reflecting on how you thought and behaved during adolescence generates undeniable understandings of your true self. Artifacts and insights from your past are pieces of your life puzzle connected to who you were, and who you still are!

Do you have journals or diaries from the past? Did you ever write a letter to yourself? Has a significant person in your life given you feedback? What would your letter to yourself at age 18 have said?

SELF ASSESSMENT 6-6: MAPPING MY LIFE STORY

Select 5-10 events or experiences you believe have shaped your life at various ages. Describe, draw, or insert pictures on this life map. Chart your rises and falls, highs and lows:

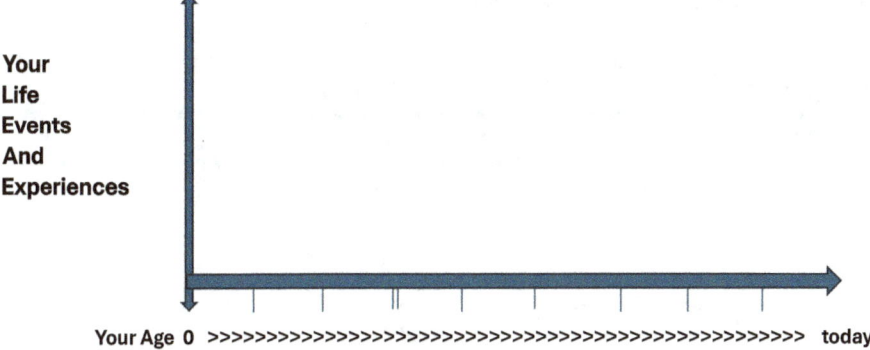

Your
Life
Events
And
Experiences

Your Age 0 >> today

Clearly identify your values and claim your moral compass
Values are shaped by the people, places, and experiences of your life. Face yourself in a mirror and admit what you stand for. Talk about the values motivating you from within. To pinpoint your highest values, revisit the life map you created. What motivated you to reach a goal or a high point? Add the whys for each phase of your journey to the chart. Reflect on the years before and after your key events. What else happened in the time leading up to the event? For the crucibles or significant emotional events, how and why did you pick yourself up and move on? Write about the inner beliefs, experiences, or people that you drew from, or were inspired by, as you recovered from a loss, overcame a challenge, or solved a serious problem. How did your values change, or become stronger[26]? Which beliefs did you bring forward with you to today? Which beliefs or values have you abandoned or adjusted?

Identify and own your capabilities, styles, strengths, and success factors
As you work on your leadership development and self-improvement, do you spend most of your time identifying weaknesses, then working to correct them? Many of us do this. Instead of trying to be someone you are not, find ways to capitalize, and build on, who you already are. Spend more time uncovering your natural talents. Focus on using your positive qualities and skills to overcome the weaknesses holding you back.

Chart your strengths using the bubble exercise below. Step back to analyze how your strengths complement each other. Reflect on how you use them (or not) at work, at home, in relationships. Which talent or strength is your genius--something you are passionate about that makes you stand apart? Do your colleagues and family members know what you are good at? Can you make even better use of your positive qualities and skills in your life and work? Think more about your personality traits. Most of these are inborn or learned at a very young age. They are a major component of who you are. Which personality traits have been useful in your life and career? What parts of your personality have held you back or hurt you?

Become a learner about yourself. Expand your conscious understanding of the information and emotions from the hidden and unknown panes of your Johari Window. Think about your layers of personality, talents, and strengths. What is their effect on your life choices? Do your choices make the best use of who you are, what you know, and what you can do?

DISCOVERY EXERCISE 6-7: A WEB OF YOUR STRENGTHS

Fill the bubbles with descriptions of what you believe are your biggest strengths or skills today. Draw lines or make notes, as appropriate, to make connections between them.

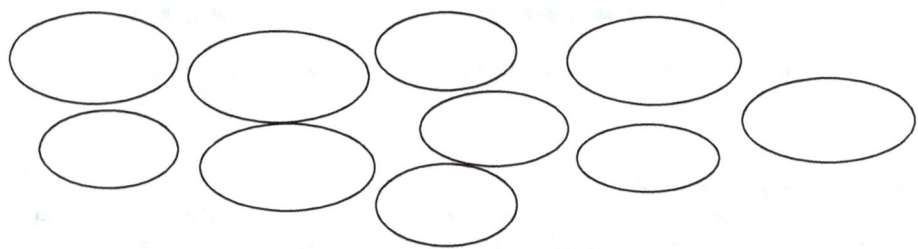

Seek authentic feedback

Learn from the authentic people in your life. These people are adamantly, yet respectfully, direct about their beliefs and their own life story. They offer opinions whether you ask or not. They keep you on track by asking piercing questions about what you do and why you do it. Make it clear to your close friends, relatives, partner, and co-workers: you welcome and encourage feedback. These trusted supporters will tell the truth(s) about you. Simply ask, then listen.

When you first hear feedback, good or bad, you may flinch, become uncomfortable, or even get upset. This is a normal reaction based on your natural fear of failure. Calmly accept critique or praise. Let some time pass before you reflect on this new information or respond to it. When you are ready, think objectively and deeply about what you heard. What did you think or feel when you received the feedback? Where is the reality or lesson for you? Somewhere in the feedback process you unearth grains of truth and more pieces of the puzzle of your unknown self. You find new ways to grow and develop as a leader.

What about those performance reviews from your manager? Are they meaningful? Do they help you gain skills and commit more to your role and your company? Do you get feedback often enough? If you go through a review process in your job, do what you can to make it useful. Learn more about what others see in you. Tell your manager you value, appreciate, and welcome feedback. Ask directly on a regular basis: How am I doing? What did I do well? What can I improve? How would you have handled that task, situation, or problem? Ask about the technical aspects and tasks of the work, as well as how you can improve teamwork and relationships. Seek reactions from your peers and followers. Encourage them to communicate courageously and to become comfortable giving, and getting, genuine feedback. Everyone on your team will gain leadership skills and become more successful.

Face your non-capabilities and weaknesses
High achievers can be perfectionists. Often, we strive for flawlessness, not for ourselves, but to please others and meet their expectations. However, perfection does not exist. It is only in the eye of the beholder! When we try to achieve it, people may shy away from working and interacting with us. To find and be your authentic self, do not chase perfection. Set realistic goals. Stop when your work is good enough. You can always improve on it later or the next time.

One of the greatest qualities of an authentic leader is readiness to embrace your shortcomings. Recognize the confines of your talents and time. Acknowledging your limitations and admitting your errors to others is at the heart of authenticity. This inner and outer humility proves you are authentic. And, as all the great inventors and neuroscientists tell us: We learn much more from our failures than our successes.

Admitting your flaws sets you free. Once you believe it is okay to have flaws and make mistakes, you can be who you are and do what you do best. You gain a sense of calm and release from within. Stay true to who you are. Be okay accepting the consequences of your faults. Regardless of your weaknesses, you will still achieve so much. Sharing our vulnerabilities and troubles with our peers, followers, and friends makes relationships stronger. People want to follow, learn from, and associate with others who are real people with human shortcomings. When we share our challenges and needs with others, we gain their trust and receive the gift of their input or advice. Everyone learns and grows together.

DISCOVERY EXERCISE 6-8: A WEB OF YOUR WEAKNESSES
Fill the bubbles with descriptions of what you believe are your biggest weaknesses or needs today. Draw lines or make notes, as appropriate, to make connections between them.

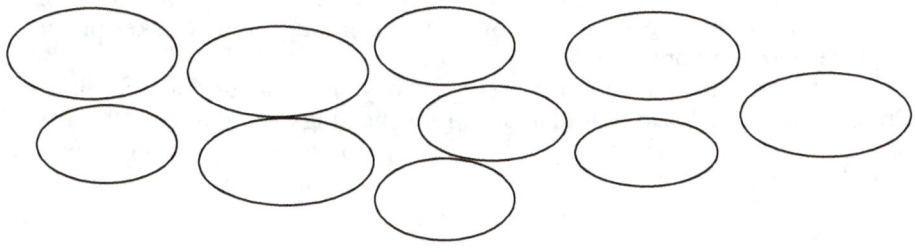

Become confident about who you are and what you can achieve
As you unravel the tangled yarns of your authentic self, find what makes you proud. What have you accomplished with your talents? Acknowledge these achievements. Give yourself credit. Stop to applaud your competencies, especially your coping skills and your abilities to recover from troubles and difficulties. Reward yourself for a job well done. Own and celebrate your stories. Recognize the skills you developed. Use the memories of your accomplishments to build confidence and become comfortable in your own skin. Above all, begin to laugh at your mistakes, and have fun with your shortcomings. Humor and playfulness help us accept ourselves and bond with others.

Over time, your repertoire of experiences, and their outcomes, converts to intuition and wisdom. These are products of your subconscious mind and its collection of knowledge and reasoning gained over time. The brain retains this data to give you quick answers and guidance in decision-making and problem-solving[27]. Trust your gut. If you make a mistake, you will learn from it, with improved insight for the future. Savor your journey. Relax, and be mindful. Do not let fears hold you back. Return to the self that is lovable and true[28]. Enjoy who you are, who you have been, what you have learned, and where you are going. Continue using your strengths, following your passions, sticking to your values, and acknowledging your failures. Love yourself, and you will lead with your heart.

Practice transparent communication, then practice again
Your evidence of authenticity is in communication, communication, and more communication. You practice authenticity in life and leadership by clearly expressing your identity and your truth to everyone you encounter. Be honest, open, genuine, and direct. Today, communication is not only what we say. It is verbal, non-verbal, written, spoken, and silently conveyed. To communicate authentically, yet effectively, is complicated. Your communications repertoire starts with your general presence. Do you exude humble self-confidence and credibility with your posture and facial expressions? To present your authentic self to others, you need advanced skills for in-person communications, written communications, online communications, and silent communications. Gaining competencies to express who you are and what you believe is situational and relational. It requires keen use of emotional intelligence and self-leadership. This seems like a daunting endeavor, and it is. When it comes to communications, we are always on a steep learning curve. It takes practice, practice, and more practice.

Take time to plan for expressing who you are and what you believe. Preparation works! Do you plan ahead for meetings and dialogues? Most of us do not. Be mindful about your upcoming communications opportunities. Think about what will be discussed. Anticipate how you will respond to the agenda items. Have a set of ideas for how you can effectively incorporate your values, beliefs, and talents.

When the stakes are high for a conversation in life or work, write down what you want to say. Formulate the message, but also the non-verbals: voice tone, facial expressions, body language, and voice volume. Carefully consider what emotions will be appropriate in the conversation. Practice out loud in front of a mirror. See how you look and what emotions you are projecting. During and after any dialogue or presentation, replay the exchange in your mind. If possible, record yourself and play it back. Listen to your voice and tone. Notice the verbals and nonverbals. Reflect on what was said and the outcomes of the dialogue. What worked? What did not work as you hoped? What might work better the next time in a similar situation? Take note. Process, analyze, and learn. Rehearse the changes in your head. Next time, practice what you learned. Do not get discouraged. Try again to be yourself, and to express your understandings and reasons. Further unfold and perfect your stories. Develop assertiveness, constructive feedback, constructive dialogue, negotiation, and conflict transformation skills. Collect a set of books or resources on difficult and advanced communications. Learn to do battle (or not) at appropriate times and places[29]. Different situations require different approaches. Remember to express your genuine knowledge, beliefs, and strengths. You will be practicing all your life. And practice begets improvement!

ASSESSMENT EXERCISE 6-9: AUTHENTICITY SKILLS & MINDSETS

Record your thoughts about how to use these tools for authenticity in your leadership. You may have more than one idea for an item. You may have no comments or ideas for others.

Authenticity Skills and Mindsets	How I Can Use This to Improve my Authenticity and Leadership
Finding truths in my life story	
Clearly identifying my values and morals	
Knowing my capabilities, styles, and strengths	
Seeking authentic feedback	
Facing my non-capabiities and weaknesses	
Confidence in who I am and what I can achieve	
Practicing transparent communications	

BEYOND THE INDIVIDUAL: AUTHENTICITY WEB OF BELIEF[SM] IN TEAMS & ORGANIZATIONS

The uncertainty created by social and organizational upheavals, along with acts of unethical and ineffective leadership, has strengthened the call for constructive and genuine approaches to serve the common good. Organizations who believe in authenticity identify corporate values and use a moral compass to frame their cultures. These organizations clearly communicate their mission and meaning. They encourage their people to learn and understand the stories and crucibles of the organization's history. The organization's structure, policies, and standards are clear, guided by ethics, and designed to generate motivation and morale. This helps employees align themselves with the values of the organization. Individuals and teams need to practice ethical leadership with respect and dignity, to bring good to others.

Authentic organizations are transparent and honest about people, capital, information, and resources. Their culture encourages trust between individuals, teams, and groups. Authenticity promotes positive psychological and ethical climates[30]. Employees are encouraged to share feelings and needs, leading to better relationships all around. All are free to perform their jobs[31]. When leaders and corporations are clear and consistent about the direction they are heading, people engage in initiatives, and goals are achieved.

Authentic leaders are needed in organizations across the world because they can function in complex environments, using different behaviors in different situations, yet maintain their direction, integrity, and credibility. They teach followers to recognize the ethical issues they face in their jobs and think about the consequences of their decisions. They courageously challenge organizational processes. By adhering to their beliefs, authentic leaders establish credibility with followers and stakeholders[32]. The values modeled by authentic leaders influence the values exhibited by everyone in the organization.

Leader integrity and credibility is key for follower trust and performance. Authentic leaders model openness and clarity as they share information. This inspires direct communication and robust dialogue[33]. Authentic leaders ask what is really going on and what is true, then act on followers' answers. When team members and leaders work together authentically, they generate ideas, address issues directly, and create shared meaning. They get to root causes of problems and find innovative solutions[34].

Authentic leaders and their organizations help build employees' self-confidence. They model the importance of self-esteem and identity because their own behaviors are consistent with their self-concept. Their teams and organizations develop a wide range of leadership competencies. When authentic leaders encourage self-leadership, followers do not need micro-management. They more readily engage in their roles and communicate transparently in problem-solving and decision-making. When employees and their managers focus on strengths, employees significantly increase their engagement[35].

THE AUTHENTICITY WEB OF BELIEF^{SM} IN ACTION

Steve Jobs: Inventor, Executive, Change Agent[36]

People who are crazy enough to change the world are the ones who do.

STEVE JOBS

After dropping out of college, Jobs became sure of who he was and what he wanted to do. He knew he had the talent and drive to transform computing and telecommunications. Jobs set out to conquer complexity in technology. He believed he could connect humanity and creativity to engineering and the sciences, and he relentlessly pursued this. He proved this to the world by creating streamlined products that were simple to use. Jobs was a master of genuine and unadulterated communication. He never apologized for his passion, emotionalism, and intensity. He always expressed and acted on his convictions about life and work. Some called him blunt and authoritative, but his teams were motivated by his honest feedback and imagination. They believed in him and came together to achieve his goals. As a leader and a marketer, he had a contagious effect on people. He built Apple to be the highest valued company in the world. When diagnosed with cancer, he transparently communicated his situation and kept working on what he loved. He would "stay hungry and stay foolish" until the end.

Jackie Robinson: Professional Athlete, Civil Rights Pacesetter, Pioneer[37]

I am not concerned with your liking or disliking me. All I ask is that you respect me as a human being.

JACKIE ROBINSON

Jackie Roosevelt Robinson was born into a family of sharecroppers but keenly understood himself and his strong athletic talent. He attended UCLA and became a superstar in four sports. He became one of the first black second lieutenants in the U.S. Army during World War II. In 1947, through his perseverance and quiet presence, Robinson led the civil rights movement to break the color barrier in Major League Baseball. He triumphed as a player to be a six-time All-Star and World Series champion. Jackie was disliked and harassed by fans and fellow baseball players, but he believed in himself and his right to play. He communicated openly and transparently about his feelings and the discrimination he faced. During times of injustice, he spoke out, led by example, and stuck to his moral compass and core beliefs. He encouraged African Americans to push for their rights and not be complacent. Jackie Robinson's life story has endured as an example and inspiration to all in baseball, sports, and those who continue to strive for equal rights. His commitment to his identity is legendary.

Dolly Parton: Musician, Entertainer, Theme Park Executive, Entertainment Executive, Philanthropist[38]

I think everybody should be allowed to be who they are, and to love who they love. Everyone has their own journey. They have their own way of doing things. And who am I to judge?
   DOLLY PARTON

Dolly Rebecca Parton came from modest beginnings: near-poverty conditions and hardship. She is, and always has been, simply herself, with authenticity as her superpower. She became one of the most successful country music singers/songwriters but is also renowned for making people feel loved and appreciated. After her leading role in the movie *9 to 5*, the world beyond country music embraced her ingenuity. Her authenticity makes her likable, charismatic, and endearing. Parton's music embodies confidence and optimism. Dolly's humble life story motivates her to invest her fortune in education, health care, and animal preservation. Her Imagination Library sends monthly books to toddlers. She established an eagle sanctuary at Dollywood, her entertainment center. She built an entertainment and business empire but declined a nomination to the Rock and Roll Hall of Fame, hoping someone more deserving would take her place. Parton has been dubbed a leadership rock star with a blueprint for leadership humility. With her resources and credibility, she is someone who will continue to make a difference in our world.

Sidney Poitier: Oscar Winning Actor, Diplomat, Change Agent[39]

It's difficult when you're carrying other peoples' dreams. And so you have to hold on to the dream that is inside yourself, and know if you are true to that, that's all that matters.
   SIDNEY POITIER

Sir Sidney Poitier communicated his convictions and principles through his art. After being rejected at an acting tryout, he changed his accent and studied successful actors. As the first African American leading man and Oscar winner, he transformed the portrayal of Blacks in movies. His classic roles in *Lilies of the Field, In the Heat of the Night, and Guess Who's Coming to Dinner* highlighted his hope to empower future generations of people of color. He lived by his principles and promoted civil rights by refusing to play cowards, servants, or entertainers. He openly insisted on respect and honorable treatment from the Press. He used his status as America's favorite actor to influence leaders in entertainment and government, becoming a civil rights activist with a very peaceful style. He was authentic, credible, and dignified. People listened to his groundbreaking advice on nonviolent integration.

CONCLUSION

Authenticity may be the secret weapon in our development as leaders. We discover who we are by learning who we have been. Our stories illuminate our self-understanding. Our values and beliefs become clear. We understand our tendencies and our talents. We honestly communicate our unique identity. Our beliefs guide our decisions and behaviors. We know how we think. We admit our weaknesses, the limits of our capabilities, and our mistakes. We do not try to, or want to, be anything or anyone we are not. We are comfortable in our own skin. We are free to be ourselves.

As authentic humans and leaders, we clearly and confidently express ourselves. Followers and peers at work, and in our lives, trust us because our stories and our actions are credible and true. We elicit openness and feedback from those we work with, those who work for us, and those we work for. This is not easy. Our journey to authenticity continues for our whole lifetime. As our stories evolve, we continue to practice our communications skills, find out what works, and practice more. We continue building strengths and skills. We learn to humbly, yet proudly and genuinely, express who we are and what we are becoming.

ADDITIONAL RESOURCES

Crucial Confrontations. Kerry Patterson, Joseph Grenny, Ron McMillan, Al Switzler. McGraw-Hill, 2005

Fearless Negotiating. Michael C. Donaldson. McGraw Hill, 2007.

How Am I Doing. Forty Conversations to Have with Yourself. Dr. Corey Yeager. Harper Celebrate, 2022

Inclusive Conversations. Mary-Frances Winters. Berrett-Koehler, 2020.

Something More: Excavating Your Authentic Self. Sara Ban Breathnach. Warner Books, 1998.

Strengths Finder 2.0: Discover Your Clifton Strengths. Don Clifton and Tom Rath. Gallup, 2017.

The Coward's Guide to Conflict. Tim Ursiny, Ph.D. Sourcebooks, Inc. 2003

The Definitive Book of Body Language. Allen and Barbara Pease. Bantam, 2004

The Six Pillars of Self-Esteem. Nathaniel Brandon. Bantam, 1994.

True North. Emerging Leader Edition. Bill George and Zach Clayton. Wiley, 2022

CHAPTER APPENDIX

The AUTHENTICITY Web of Belief℠	Competencies & Mindsets Developed Within Leadership Theories and Styles
Complexity/Strategic/ Adaptive/Crisis/Executive Leadership Capacities	Broad behavioral repertoire, social intelligence, charismatic leadership, lead in context, provide encouragement, resources, multi-level adaptivity, enabling leadership, behavioral complexity, transformational leadership[40], strengthen transparency, communicate actively[41], take responsibility for decisions, take responsibility for communications [42]
Shared/Connective/ Servant/ Team/Leadership and Followership Capacities	Social awareness, empathy, social skills. building bonds, conflict management, friendship, inquiry, generative dialogue, enable, empower, leader-member exchange, integrity, name and shape identity, maximize interactions, entrust, social skills, networking, persuasive, transparent, open, information sharing, frequent communication, attribution of meaning in communications, advanced interpersonal skills, extroversion, conflict overcoming, make new connections, strengthen connections, vulnerability[43], team self-observation, team self-talk, feedback, team beliefs and assumptions[44], challenge leaders[45], transformative, persuasive[46], challenge the process, encourage the heart [47]
Authentic Leadership/ Self Leadership/Emotional Intelligence Capacities	Self-awareness, self-clarity, self-certainty of values and identity, personal and social identification, self-knowledge, receiving feedback, reflective circumspection of life stories, authentic behavior, positive emotions, other-directed emotions, positive modeling, emotional contagion, person-role merger, relational transparency, positive psychological capital, act with personal values and convictions, have a distinct voice, multiple, contradictory roles and behaviors with integrity, internalized moral perspective[48], relational transparency, charisma, values, trust[49], work to be more open, courage, take calculated risks, stand up for what you believe, political skills through experience, influence skills, debate, self-efficacy, reciprocity, reduce discrepancies, find opportunities in failure, use negative feedback to your advantage[50]
Change Leadership & Transformational Leadership Capacities	Credibility, direction, inspirational, communicative, balanced processing, unbiased, communicate clear vision[51], persevere and persist[52], model the way, challenge the process, encourage the heart[53], individualized consideration, idealized influence, transformative, persuasive, positive psychology[54]

FINDING FLÂNEUR

Storms rise around us.
We endure, and they subside.
As leaders, we must pause to find
our inspiration and essence.
Like the rivers,
where we meander,
and how we adapt our course,
will lead us to a gentle and graceful flow.

PAT O'CONNELL

CHAPTER 7

THE FLÂNEUR WEB OF BELIEF^{SM}

> Belief in a philosophical, multi-perspective, and spirit-led approach to living and leading, balancing active participation with timely practice of observation, rest, reflection, and detachment.

WHAT IS FLÂNEUR IN THE 21ST CENTURY?

An old, French concept
Flâneur (pronounced flah- nure′) is a French noun meaning stroller or saunterer. The concept of flâneur was given broader meaning in 19th century French literature when many rural people moved to the new, industrialized city of Paris from the quiet and beautiful farmlands. They found the city noisy, crowded, smelly, and chaotic compared to their bucolic countryside. A *flâneur* came to mean a person who could experience and understand the city by walking it and observing it[1]. The poet Baudelaire explained flâneur as a philosophical way to live, think, and understand, while remaining a detached observer[2].

Valuable for leadership
Flâneur was introduced in the early 21st century as a mindset and skillset for leadership. Leaders today struggle to find a sense of calm in a world of chaos. They use flâneur to become quiet and reflective, yet still passionately engaged in the noisy environments of their work and life. Flâneur in leadership comprises detachment, observation, reflection, reasoning, and contemplation to gain insight and intuition[3].

Balancing action (engagement) with inaction (observation)
Baudelaire described a flâneur as one who could find joy and peace in the ebb and flow of the movement around them. To be a flâneur meant maintaining balance by interspersing periods of action with inaction. In our fast-paced world, it is easy to get caught in a perpetual cycle of work, to-do lists, obligations, and the constant stimulation of electronics. Leaders can use flâneur to thoughtfully navigate the conflicts and commotion of daily life.

Thinking carefully before acting
John Dewey, famous educational philosopher, described reflection as a unique approach to thinking in which we doubt, hesitate, and question what we are

experiencing or doing. Dewey's practice of purposeful inquiry challenges us to change and improve what we already know. He advocated reflection to critique our actions, test new ideas, and re-consider our responses to situations[4].

No matter how uncontrolled their environment seems, today's leaders must step back to gain perspective. They need to objectively respond and adapt to vulnerability, uncertainty, chaos, and continuous change. Using flâneur, they gain new insight about what is, and what is not, going on around them. They focus on being, rather than doing.

FLÂNEUR IN LEADER DEVELOPMENT: THE FLÂNEUR WEB OF BELIEF[SM]

The fifth web of belief for leader development is flâneur. Flâneur involves slowing down the body and mind to become spectators of our environment. We take time for periods of peacefulness and rest. We use self-reflection to learn from our life stories and leadership experiences. We become adept at calmly navigating the challenges, pressures, and problems we encounter in life and career. Using flâneur, leaders pause to simply observe. We take time to gain perspective. A leader practicing flâneur remains interested and involved but steps back to assess a situation. We allow time to process information more deeply. We are detached and mindful, yet passionate, observers[5].

The Flâneur Web of Belief requires leaders to synthesize information from our surroundings. We stop to question ourselves and others. We determine what we are thinking and feeling before we act. The practices of perspective-taking and reflective questioning help us respond to paradoxes and contradictions. The contemplation and deliberation associated with flâneur bridges the gaps between people and builds practical wisdom[6].

Once we make observations and try to better understand, we can react thoughtfully to people and situations. We improve how we receive and process information for greater perspective, more creativity, and better problem solving[7]. Leaders with flâneur are purposeful and effective in decisions and actions. We prioritize what is truly important in our life and work and manage our time accordingly. We improve how we receive and process information for more creative problem solving. We take action that is timely and smart. Competencies for flâneur include coping with stress and balancing personal and professional pursuits. We prioritize our mental and physical health and work toward work-life balance. We understand the connections between mind, body, and spirit.

When leaders intersperse periods of intense focus with periods of rest and detachment, we significantly improve our ability to function at peak levels. We are more productive at work and at home. Leaders using flâneur navigate increasingly complex situations and interactions over the career and the life span. We become more self-aware and mindful. We manage our time. We reduce stress and confusion. We enjoy a healthier lifestyle.

REFLECTION ACTIVITY 7-1: THE FLÂNEUR WEB OF BELIEF IN YOUR LIFE

Using the definition of the Flâneur Web of Belief, note where and how you are using it.

Aspects of the Flâneur Web of Belief	How I do this at work	How I do this at home	How I can practice this in the future
I take a philosophical and spirit-led approach			
I balance participation with observation			
I balance rest with activity			
I reflect on my life and work			

UNDERSTANDING THE FLÂNEUR WEB OF BELIEF[SM]

21st century life and work are busy, chaotic, and complex. There is pressure to get much done in little time. Flâneur involves taking time for observation and consideration before acting, to focus on our *being* rather than our *doing*.

It is about observing ourselves and our environments

The best decision making and problem-solving processes use root cause analysis to determine what happened and what is needed before identifying alternatives for solutions and next steps. Likewise, our interpersonal relations and leadership practices need consideration and evaluation. Flâneurs in literature observed their surroundings carefully yet calmly before taking action.

Passionate observation is standing back to perceive what is happening in our world. We become quiet. We clear our minds. We avoid distractions and use body language to show we are paying close attention. We absorb what we hear and see. We gather information and facts without presumption. We defer judgment and response[8]. We stop to listen, then think, then seek to understand.

Leadership Case: The Paradox of Flâneur

> Flâneur may seem like a strange concept. It is a French word, rarely used in other languages. The essence of flâneur is calm, rest, and reflection. Yet, to achieve a state of flâneur, we work intensely to balance work and life, manage our time, and take time out to think and recuperate. We passionately observe and listen to our surroundings. This takes quiet, deep attention. Flâneur is a complex mix of hard and soft skills. It ranges from meditation to time management. Leading and living with flâneur is a paradox. Being a flâneur is challenging. Leaders use persistence and resilience to pursue flâneur through their stages of adulthood.
>
> *How does practicing flâneur become a paradox or a challenge in your life and work?*

It's about learning to reflect

Maybe reflective practices offer us a way of trying to make sense of the uncertainty in our workplaces and the courage to work competently and ethically at the edge of order and chaos.

TONY GHAYE[9]

Reflective practice was introduced in the 1980's to improve workplace proficiency. Studies of professionals using reflective practice find they achieve higher expertise in their discipline compared to those who do not reflect. In problem solving, reflection improves understanding and leads to more creative solutions. In interpersonal leadership, we use it to make sense of our interactions, then adjust our behaviors for better results[10].

Reflection is a form of analysis and evaluation, directed within, and by, oneself. We use our powers of metacognition, or thinking about our own thinking and experience, to interpret our world. We learn to reflect on our actions after events to gain insight for future practice. We also develop skills for reflection *in action*, evaluating situations while they occur[11]. Based on our understandings and conclusions, we carefully plan next steps.

For active reflection, we use journaling, counseling, training, or mentoring. Passive reflection includes meditation and mindfulness. Reflection takes time, but it ultimately saves time and energy because we make more effective decisions. Using contemplation and deliberation accelerates development of self-awareness and social awareness. We are more thoughtful and peaceful in our approach to life and work.

Questioning ourselves and others

Thinking is a process of questioning, and questioning is an orderly form of reflective thinking. Self-questioning means asking ourselves about the past, present, and future. We wonder about our habits and our feelings. This question-and-answer process is creative. We investigate new ideas and find new aspects of what we already know. We increase our understanding of ourselves, our surroundings, and our relationships[12]. Through self-questioning, we pause to monitor and regulate. We clarify our purpose, better use our strengths, and improve on our weaknesses. As we improve our flâneur, we build confidence and become more optimistic.

Appreciative inquiry uses the power of questioning for positive discovery and creative decision-making. Its purpose is to build shared meaning amongst individuals and focus on positive future outcomes. Problems and differences of opinion are explored using affirmative and cooperative language. We compose questions to encourage and inspire, not to blame or punish. Appreciative questions are worded to identify the best of what is and what can be. They focus on strengths, opportunities, and advantages[13]. Team members answer these questions with authentic responses. As a result, they reach mutual understanding and find ways to collaborate. Problem solving is more effective and relationships improve.

Leadership Lesson: Wicked Problems and Wicked Questions[14]

Our world is fraught with unique social and cultural difficulties to overcome --poverty, access to education, war amongst nations, sustainability, healthcare, recycling, and climate change. These are challenging dilemmas, seemingly impossible to resolve. Problems are wicked when they have complicated layers. To seek solutions, we must unwind the coils of complexity surrounding them and address the underlying issues. Entire systems need innovation and redesign to make progress toward solving wicked problems. Wicked questions are complex questions with many possible answers. They are often phrased as a paradox. Addressing wicked problems and wicked questions compels us to forge bold, creative, and vigorous plans. An example of a wicked question:

How can I be fully engaged in my career, yet at the same time available and dedicated to my family? What are your answers to this paradoxical question?

To gain perspective, awareness, and mindfulness

Slowing down our minds and bodies to reflect on our actions and behaviors makes us think deeper, broader, and more clearly. We have sharper focus and refined attention to events within and outside ourselves. We understand better the complexities of our environment and the meaning of thoughts and actions. We use a nonjudgmental lens. We become calm in the face of crisis, chaos, vulnerability, uncertainty, and change. We regulate our behavior and avoid detrimental or negative responses. We increase our reasoning powers for decision making in work and life[15].

Using flâneur, we become mindful and present in the moment. Calming the mind reduces physical symptoms of stress and prevents stress-related illnesses[16]. We gain a sense of personal control over a situation, reducing frustration and negativity. Scientific studies show soothing our mental activity can contribute to well-being, hope, optimism, and creativity. We forge better relationships and find more satisfaction in work and life.

To work toward healthful, balanced living

The demands of our work and our world can lead to unhealthy habits. We are driven to be highly productive and constantly achieving. We absorb at least five times more information each day than we did just 50 years ago. 24/7 electronic messaging and global communication keep us always on-call. Our boundaries blur, creating work-life fusion[17]. We become frustrated and overloaded. We reach a point of diminishing returns, even burnout, as we work harder, not smarter. These stressors contribute to health risks, low performance, and even death.

Using the Flâneur Web of Belief involves balancing our work and life to lessen the stress sustained by our mind, body, and spirit. To be balanced leaders, we need to match daily living choices with our personal values. Interspersing periods of rest with contemplation helps us identify what is most important in our life. Acting on our priorities and beliefs relieves stress and contributes to our flâneur. Finding balance does not always mean slowing down. In personal or professional pursuits, being in "flow" involves taking on challenges just beyond our current capabilities. Examples are staying up late to finish a good book; putting in extra time to complete an engaging work project; or working to reach a new level of achievement in a video game. Pursuing activities to reach a state of flow generates satisfaction, enthusiasm, energy, and happiness for individuals and groups[18]. We have more control over our lives, and we even live longer.

Leadership Case: Are We Ever in Perfect Balance?

No matter how hard we work at it, balance in life is elusive. We are always in the process of balancing and re-balancing. As we move through stages of life, our circumstances, work, personal interests, family responsibilities, and values change. Our interests and talents evolve. The ratio of time for job, family, personal interests, and rest varies at different career and life phases. What we value at each stage influences our balance. We may shift from work-centric to family-centric to self-centric. Using the Flâneur Web of Belief, we stay aware of our needs and recalibrate our scales of balance.

Can you recall a moment or period in your life when you felt in close-to-perfect balance? Describe the circumstances and the situation.

REFLECTION 7-2: MY WORK/LIFE BALANCE

Answer these questions:

Describe your stage of life
Describe your stage of career/work
What is your current work/life balance reality and why?
What is practical and probable for your work/life balance during this time of life and career?
What are your hopes or wishes for finding better work/life balance?

To act and live wisely

Using reflection-in-action and reflection-on-action, leaders conscientiously gather information, evaluate alternatives, and make decisions. We gain insight about people, events, and problems. We find what does and does not work for us. Our perceptions sharpen, and we apply what we learn to new situations. Our critical thinking and problem-solving skills improve. We choose sensible directions and behaviors. We gain what is called practical wisdom. We also gain intuition or *knowing in action.* Intuition is the crystallized result of our vast accumulation of experiences. It is perception, judgment, or decision making without conscious analysis. As we continue to think about our own thinking and actions, we gain intuitive powers. We become more creative in imagining possibilities and more confident in our judgments[19].

Practical wisdom about the fundamentals of life is always passed down through generations, from grandparents to parents, to children and grandchildren. It is also useful in the workplace. Practical wisdom involves social skills, emotional regulation, empathy, compassion, self-reflection, acceptance of uncertainty, decisiveness, moral judgment, and spirituality. Neurobiologists and psychologists find we develop practical wisdom by viewing our experiences and life events through a lens that transcends the self[20]. Using flâneur, we step away to observe our actions and their consequences. We become wise about how to live well.

REFLECTION 7-3: YOUR FLÂNEUR TODAY

Describe two recent situations in which you lost your calm, showed frustration, talked instead of listened, or interrupted someone.

1.
2.

How could you have used flâneur to improve your interaction and/or improve your leadership in those settings?

1.
2.

LEADER COMPETENCIES & STYLES WITHIN THE FLÂNEUR WEB OF BELIEF^{SM}

Self-leadership and emotional intelligence competencies

Leaders using the Flâneur Web of Belief gain expertise in self-leadership. These leaders become keenly aware of themselves in relation to their surroundings. They observe and reflect on their own values, identity, and actions. They use this information to improve their reasoning processes and understand their limitations. Practicing flâneur, leaders work through inner obstacles to adjust their behaviors in various environments. Flâneur improves the emotional intelligence characteristics of self-awareness and self-regulation. As leaders find meaning in their lived experiences, they consider the causes and effects for their emotions and behaviors. They reflect on their responses to the stimuli around them[21]. They exercise control over their thinking and actions.

Transformational leadership and change leadership competencies
In transformational leadership and change leadership, flâneur teaches leaders to step back, question their assumptions, analyze their mindsets and behaviors, and take new perspectives. They use reflection and questioning to intellectually stimulate followers to shift their thinking and actions[22]. This in turn engages followers, fosters their development, and encourages objectivity.

Calm deliberation during a change initiative dissipates the stress of change for both leaders and followers. Active listening, reflection, and reflective questioning facilitate information gathering. Using appreciative inquiry, leaders and followers adapt to change with forward-looking plans. Leaders with flâneur objectively observe people before, during, and after changes are implemented. They adjust plans to maintain momentum for action initiatives. When leaders use active listening and reflection in change management, coalitions form, shared understanding improves, and change is longer lasting.

Crisis leadership, adaptive leadership, and complexity leadership competencies
Adaptive and complexity leaders ask wicked questions, bring unseen details to light. They reflect on the situation and listen actively to gain understanding and make new connections. Using the Flâneur Web of Belief, leaders reflect on what is and what could be. To fill the spaces between themselves and their followers, they facilitate the development of shared understandings[23]. As leaders gain practical wisdom, they use their experience and intuition to solve complex problems and recommend actions.

Leaders with flâneur first detach and distance themselves from a crisis. They stand back before they communicate and drive toward actionable intelligence[24]. They use knowing-in-action to identify challenges, analyze problems, and make decisions. With active listening and reflective questioning, they engage followers in idea generation and stress-test assumptions. When they adjust processes or implement solutions, they manage creative tension and resolve conflicts, then coordinate new initiatives.

Connective leadership, shared leadership, servant leadership, team leadership, and followership competencies
Shared and connective leaders practice passionate observation to show empathy and stewardship[25]. They adjust their lens, engaging followers in reflective dialogue to identify needs and build collaborative environments. When team leaders and servant leaders practice flâneur to calmly listen and understand, followers become more committed. This builds high-performing teams and mission-driven communities[26]. Leaders and followers who reflect before acting are more foresighted, inspirational, and optimistic.

SELF ASSESSMENT 7-4: WHAT ARE YOUR STRESSORS?

For each emotion, fill in activities, people, places, and situations that trigger this feeling in you. You may not have answers for every emotion.

My Triggers of Stressful Emotions	My Triggers of Peaceful Emotions
Anxiety	Calm
Depression	Joy
Worry	Happiness
Fear	Awe
Frustration	Kindness
Sadness	Interest
Jealousy	Contentment
Confusion	Love
Irritation	Pride
Contempt	Gratitude
Anger	Hope
Shame	Amusement
Loneliness	Inspiration
Other:	Other:
Other:	Other:

HOW TO APPLY THE FLÂNEUR WEB OF BELIEF[SM] IN YOUR LEADER DEVELOPMENT

Peace is silent. Peace is reflective and calm. Peace comes from beauty and love. Peace comes from within you.
            PAT O'CONNELL

For some developing leaders, behaviors associated with flâneur come naturally. Individuals with Type B personalities, for example, are known to be relaxed, laid back, and careful about their actions and reactions. For more active, competitive, and intense personalities, flâneur mindsets and behaviors can be challenging and elusive. For all leaders, learning flâneur is a life-long project to work toward practicing observation, reflection, and calm.

Slow down to detach and be mindful

The passionate observation of a flâneur means pausing to see, hear, and understand. To practice flâneur, calm and quiet the brain and the body. Lower your shoulders. Breathe more slowly and deeply. Relax your face and neck. Listen. Use all your senses. Tune in to your body language. Become fully present in the moment. Open your eyes, mind, and heart to what you are experiencing. As we listen and pay attention, we gain insight. We recognize patterns and make connections for creative problem solving. Force yourself to carefully construct solutions and responses. Uncover new mindsets and behaviors for your leadership.

During times of negative thinking or feelings, stop. Slow down and detach. Breathe. Calm your facial expressions. Quietly observe. Use all your senses to become mindful. Deter any worries about the past or the future. Sort out what is important, distracting, and trivial. Think clearly and regain your positive mindset. Use the Flâneur Web of Belief in every phase of life and work to act calmly and wisely. Even those around you will become more relaxed and composed.

Become a present and passionate listener
In its simplest form, flâneur is about paying attention. We often distort and misinterpret what we hear and see because we filter information through our own knowledge and beliefs. Our emotions distract us. Our mind wanders. Active listening shows interest, care, and concern. It reduces interpersonal conflict and improves relationships. Others feel valued. We take in more information and solve problems more effectively.

Listen actively. Clear your mind. Put aside distracting thoughts and feelings. Give the situation your undivided attention. Engage fully, but without judgment or interpretation. Use positive or neutral facial expressions. The cardinal rule of active listening is *do not interrupt the speaker*. Allow gaps and silences. Observe words, feelings, actions, and body language. Acknowledge the message as it is delivered. Do not think about what to say next. When it is time to speak, do not analyze, state your opinion, or give advice. Instead, respond by repeating what you heard. Ask questions to clarify your observations and understanding. Take time to understand and process what you learned before choosing how to respond or react.

Reflectively question yourself and others
In your dialogue with another, the answer may be a question[29]. When observing a situation or solving problems, think first of questions, not answers or solutions. Become aware of your questioning style. Some styles are appropriate and effective; others weaken your credibility and relationships. For example, do not ask rhetorical questions, or questions which already include an answer, because that answer may state your opinion. Leaders using this questioning style may disengage or offend followers, who may then withhold further information or ideas.

Two questioning styles for practicing flâneur are reflective questioning and appreciative inquiry. Reflective questions are open-ended and nonjudgmental. They gather information, clarify a problem, or gain insight. Reflective questioning is a high-level leadership skill. It involves the critical thinking principles of seeking clarity, depth, breadth, and perspective. It shows others you are listening, observing, and trying to understand. Use reflective questions to gather more information and clarify communications. To compose a reflective question, stop to cogitate about the situation, then inquire about why, when, where, who, and what is involved. Ask open-ended questions. Encourage followers and team members to do the same. After all questions are exhausted and answered, begin to identify options and solutions.

Appreciative inquiry brings people together to discover how they agree, along with the visions and values they share. It uses optimistic, positive, and forward-looking questions to address problems and make plans. Analyze problems by asking what could be, or what should be, rather than what went wrong. Find out what is working and what can work, rather than what did not work or who did not perform properly[30]. Use appreciative inquiry for brainstorming, strategic thinking, and decision making. Train yourself to question with wonder and optimism, not with opinion or blame. Listen to your voice volume, tone, and intonations when you ask questions. Be mindful and listen actively when your questions are answered.

Reflective Questioning and Appreciative Inquiry

The chart below gives examples and starting points for reflective and appreciative questioning.

Reflective Self Questions[31]	Reflective Questions to Others[32]	Appreciative Inquiry Questions[33]
Something is happening that surprises me. It is not usual, but what is it about?	Did you mean … (paraphrase or summarize)	What is working and what is not working in this situation?
Is what I am doing appropriate at this moment?	I'm not sure if I understand what you are saying about…	How can we improve?
Do I need to change what I am doing to adjust to changing?	How did that make you feel?	What outcomes do we really want?
If I am not on the right track, is there a better way of doing this?	What did you do next?	What actions will we value?
What is my point of view on this issue?	Would you like to hear my suggestions?	What could be done?
What is my purpose?	What is your goal?	What should be done?
What information will answer my question?	Did I answer what you were asking?	What can we do?
How can I get back in balance?	What can I do to help?	What approaches can will work for us?

Learn to disengage
Taking breaks is biologically restorative. Naps are even better.
DANIEL J. LEVITIN[34]

Humans perform better if they intersperse periods of activity with periods of rest. Leaders must find a rhythm between intense effort and unhurried relaxation. Being idle, slow, or even lazy is healthful, not sinful, in our pursuit of balance[35]. When working, take breaks for mental and physical recovery every 90 minutes. A ten-minute nap improves cognitive function and renews your energy [36]. You can also find calm, relief from stress, and mindfulness by changing your activity or your venue. Take time out to read a news article or a chapter of a book. Listen to music or a podcast. Play an electronic game, or do a puzzle. Draw, paint, or doodle. Walk across the room. Go outside. Changing your focus or taking a break for 5 -10 minutes resets your emotions and slows your reactions. Stress, anxiety, and fear subside. Use the principles of calm detachment and observation to step back from stressful situations, take care of feelings in a positive way, and regain balance.

Master the art of reflection
The process of reflection is calmly and creatively re-living what you have said or done. It is an orderly form of thinking, in which you connect meaning from one experience or idea to the next for deeper understanding. You generate new awareness and process your emotions[37]. Thoughtful contemplation is your most direct route to self-awareness and self-leadership. Use regular reflection to analyze problems and think about possibilities. As you reflect, consider ways to control your emotional reactions, test new behavior patterns, and become more empathetic.

To start a reflection, become calm and mindful. Review and reconsider an event. Remember what you were thinking and feeling. Be honest and objective about your behaviors and emotions[38]. Allow yourself to be surprised, puzzled, or confused. What did you do? What did you say? What were you thinking? How did you feel? How did others respond (or not)? Evaluate the good, and the not-so-good, about the experience. What worked? What would, or could, you do differently? In a similar situation in the future, will you do the same? What did you learn? What could you change? Consider the situation in comparison to your past thoughts, feelings, and actions. Generate new understandings. Envision creative options for improving your behavior or response.

EXERCISE 7-5: PRACTICE YOUR REFLECTION TECHNIQUES

To improve your art of reflection, complete the following exercise. For each answer, you must write at least two sentences. For some, this will be easy, and you may have more than two sentences to record. Others will struggle to keep thinking and writing about the situation. In either case, use these questions to reflect as thoroughly as you can, and keep building your skills for self-reflection.

Think of something which challenged you recently:	
Describe the situation:	
Describe what you did or have done to address this challenge (or not):	
Describe how you felt at the time:	
Describe how you feel about it now:	

What did you learn from the situation?	
What more can you learn from the situation?	
How did you respond to or resolve the challenge?	
How do you feel about your response or planned response?	
How will you address a similar challenge in the future?	

Use coping strategies

Leaders must find effective methods to deal with stress and difficulties in life and work. Use coping skills and strategies to understand problems and control your emotions. Learn more about the problem at hand and how to solve it. Positively reappraise the situation. Seek support. Set clear boundaries. Practice relaxation techniques. Exercise. Confront people and issues constructively. Change your venue, or imagine a change, to an activity, place, or person that will relieve your stress. Engage in a challenging task to block out concerns and anxieties. You will feel better and perform better.

Connect with nature

Nature is a calming and quieting force. Take a moment to turn away from work, a challenge, or a problem. Look outside. Even better, go outside. Focus on nature. Reflect on the time of year and the weather. Look at the trees and flowers. Listen to the birds, the wind, and the rain. Study the clouds and the sky. As you commute to work or to an activity, notice your natural surroundings: gardens, forests, and fields. Noticing these wonders distracts you from responsibilities, to-do lists, worries, and fears[39]. Connect with nature to re-balance your thoughts and your emotions.

Ponder and meditate

Have you ever remembered something you were supposed to do while you were in the shower, driving down the road, or waiting for an appointment? These are all forms of daydreaming. When we daydream, we detach from the task at hand. Allow yourself, even force yourself, to daydream. Quiet your mind and calm your body. Let your thoughts wander. Ignore distractions. Absorb information. Remember and imagine. Fresh ideas percolate. New patterns of thought form. You feel relaxed, refreshed, and motivated[40].

For centuries, meditation has been practiced in Eastern cultures for enlightenment and higher consciousness. Many spiritual traditions, notably the Buddhist, Hindu, Islamic, and Franciscan traditions, encourage meditation to balance periods of action in the world with contemplation and rest. Christianity encourages focus on the Bible, prayer, and singing as times for reflection and renewal. Meditation practices are now endorsed around the globe. They calm restlessness, reduce anxiety, manage depression and pain, lower blood pressure, and regulate hormones[41]. To develop the calm and mindfulness of flâneur, learn about different methods of meditation--focusing on breathing; repeating a mantra; or sitting silently in a quiet place. Find a technique that trains your mind to be present and relaxed. Create a state of inner and outer stillness to strengthen your mindfulness.

Spirituality is the recognition of an inner being that nourishes us and develops us. Community service and volunteer work also feed the inner self by providing energizing and healthful breaks from other responsibilities. Extend your search for meaning to understand your soul and your spirit. Find higher purposes in your life events. Use flâneur to cultivate your spirituality.

Leadership Case: How Meditation Became Mainstream[42]

Meditation is 2,600 years old, introduced by Buddha as a practice for awakening. Western cultures discovered it in the 18th century, but it did not gain widespread popularity until the late 20th century. When the Massachusetts Medical Center began its Mindfulness-Based Stress Reduction program in 1979, meditation was considered alternative or counter-cultural in the West. Over 500 scientific studies since 1995 find meditation practices beneficial for mental health and pain management, making mindfulness and meditation mainstream and big business in the West. Today, over 3,000 meditation techniques are promoted and sold through apps, podcasts, books, and training programs. Surely, one of these styles will work for you!

What is your plan to incorporate mindfulness into your daily routine?

Write about yourself

Journaling is an extraordinary way to improve your capacity for flâneur. Handwriting (versus keyboarding) is the most powerful method of reflection because it crosses the hands over the center of the body, activating both your left and right brain[43]. Creativity, deep insight, and recall increase. Reflection becomes deeper, broader, and more actionable if it is written.

Use regular journaling to sort out what is happening in your world. Make journaling part of your daily or weekly routine to record and organize your thoughts and feelings. You make sense of events. You process questions. You become calmer and more balanced. You discover why you think and react as you do. You set healthy intentions. You deepen your thinking and find more meaning in your life. Your practical wisdom and intuition grow. Your performance in tasks and relationships improves.

Pursue balance and well being

Leaders are more effective if they are balanced human beings. Flâneur includes focus on personal well-being to achieve work and life satisfaction, quality relationships, financial stability, physical health, and community connection. Becoming more balanced increases energy, relieves stress, and makes you feel more accomplished. It improves your productivity, problem-solving skills, and resilience[44].

Start by doing meaningful work. Find work you enjoy and believe in. Be sure your workplace and its culture fit your values and career goals. Create your own definition for success. Develop a network of valued and supportive colleagues. Beyond the workplace, nurture your body, mind, and spirit. Make work-life balance one of your highest priorities. Know when to rest and detach. Engage in leisure and social activities. Take vacations. Connect regularly with family and friends. Deepen your relationships. Do physical exercise. Eat and sleep well. Practice self-care. Notice signals of pain or illness. Manage your use of devices and technology. Nurture your mind and spirit. Being in balance is a secret weapon for accomplishing your long-term goals.

SELF ASSESSMENT 7-6: WHAT ARE YOUR STRESS RELIEVERS?

Note when and how you can use these activities to relieve stress.

Exercise
Meditation
Taking a Walk
Napping
Day Dreaming
Puzzling or Gaming
Writing
Drawing or Painting
Breathing Slowly
Talking to a Friend
Journaling
Other:
Other:

Choose how to use your time

Flâneur is about how you orchestrate the rhythm of your life. You have the same allocation of time as everyone on the globe: 24 hours for 365 days each year. You are at the helm in your journey through life. Use your free will to choose what to do with your gift of time. Be sure your activities fit your purpose and your values. Focus on what is necessary and what satisfies you. Set limits. Let the rest go. Know you will not get everything done every day. Do what makes you calm, happy, and healthy.

Explore websites, podcasts, and books with tools and tricks for time management. Find a system that works for you. Track your time to be sure you are doing what aligns with your goals. Work and play smarter, not harder. Choose meaningful and enjoyable service and leisure activities. Where and how you spend your time and direct your attention speaks volumes about who you are and what you believe.

SELF ASSESSMENT 7-7: ABOUT YOUR JOB

List items about your job in the columns, then answer the summary questions below.

What I enjoy about my job	What I do not like about my job

Develop your practical wisdom

As you practice flâneur, your thinking and actions become refined. You gain capacities for self-regulation and self-reflection. You learn to balance your emotions with your behaviors. You develop your own brand of leadership expertise. You gain practical wisdom. Calmly and confidently trust the intuition, problem-solving, and decision-making powers you develop. Draw from your practical experiences and your reflective powers. Detach, observe, reflect. Sharpen your questioning skills. Believe in your abilities to be creative and wise. Learn flâneur to balance the scales of your life. Live life passionately, yet peacefully. Enjoy the sights along the way as you journey to your destinations.

ASSESSMENT EXERCISE 7-8: FLÂNEUR SKILLS & MINDSETS

Record your thoughts about how to use these tools for authenticity in your leadership. You may have more than one idea for an item. You may have no comments or ideas for others.

Flâneur Skills and Mindsets	How I Can Use This to Improve my Flâneur and Leadership
Slowing down to detach and be mindful	
Becoming a present and passionate listener	
Reflectively questioning myself and others	
Learning to disengage	
Mastering the art of reflection	
Using coping strategies	
Connecting with nature	
Pondering and meditating	

Write about yourself	
Pursuing balance and well-being	
Choosing how to use my time	
Developing practical wisdom	

BEYOND THE INDIVIDUAL: THE FLÂNEUR WEB OF BELIEF[SM] IN TEAMS & ORGANIZATIONS

Change is more successful when organizations adopt principles of flâneur to promote deep thinking, careful decision-making, and cohesive team building. Using reflective practices, individuals and teams gain communications skills, find their voice, and become positive role models. Encouraging everyone to observe, detach, analyze, and consider alternatives promotes better communications and robust decision-making.

Using flâneur, high performing teams engage in constructive dialogue. Team members calmly address uncertainty, chaos, change, and crisis. Active listening and reflective questioning about issues and challenges contributes to deeper understanding, shared meaning making, and creative problem solving[45]. When teams use appreciative inquiry to identify organizational problems and opportunities, they generate innovative ideas, shared values, and shared bonds. When strategic planning processes use appreciative inquiry, teams develop growth mindsets and forward-looking change initiatives. Individuals and groups improve their critical thinking and practical wisdom.

Organizations who understand the benefits of flâneur establish a culture in which health and well-being are prioritized. They recognize the stress of demanding workloads, staff shortages, job insecurity, and the challenge of balancing work and life. Organizations using the Flâneur Web of Belief institute supportive practices like creative or flexible scheduling, virtual work opportunities, fitness centers and sports facilities, healthy food on-site, life skills and financial counseling, time off for family needs, parental leave, community childcare, mental health support, mindfulness workshops, and community service. They provide adequate human resources support, effective training programs, career planning, and inclusion initiatives to cultivate employees with healthy minds, bodies, and spirits[46]. These practices encourage creativity and innovation to benefit individuals, organizations, and societies.

Organizational leaders practicing flâneur model well-being and prescribe reasonable workloads. They encourage people to detach, rest, and rejuvenate by taking breaks. They understand the benefits of keeping employees happy, healthy, and engaged. They may foster a spiritual mindset in the workplace, and help employees find meaning in their lives. When individuals reduce stress and learn to work carefully and calmly, they gain courage and confidence to be their complete selves. They are productive, satisfied, and committed. The organization achieves long-term financial health. Morale improves, and the best and brights people stay[47].

THE FLÂNEUR WEB OF BELIEF[SM] IN ACTION

Volodymyr Zelenskyy: Political Leader, Entertainer, Diplomat[48]

The fight is here. I need ammunition, not a ride.
VOLODYMYR ZELENSKYY

Volodymyr Oleksandrovych Zelenskyy studied law to be a diplomat, but by happenstance wandered into a first career as a comedian and actor. He enjoyed his time as an entertainer, and patiently waited for an opportune time to enter politics. As 6th President of Ukraine, he vowed to reform the corrupt government, but soon became the leader of a nation at war with Russia. He did not flinch or despair. He simply went to work to build hope for his people and manage the intricacies of the war. His optimism and charisma help him to find order in chaos every day. After several years at war, he remains non-plussed. His demeanor and his message do not waiver. He handles every act against him with grace and ease. He faces impossible odds with dignity. He regularly finds time to visit leaders around the world with a clear and consistent message and plea for help to defeat Ukraine's aggressors. His practical wisdom is evident as he calmly deals with every new attack and setback. President Zelenskyy remains assured of his vision of peaceful independence. He uses mindfulness to keep his message clear. He finds footing on uncertain ground. As he deals with the chaos of an unending war, he continues to challenge oligarchs and fight corruption in his government. He simply rolls up his sleeves and keeps hope alive each day. He shows us how to deal with a wicked problem using finesse and flâneur.

Herb Kelleher: Business CEO, Innovator[49]

We will hire someone with less experience, less education, and less expertise, than someone who has more of those things and has a rotten attitude. Think small and act small, and we'll get bigger. Think big and act big, and we'll get smaller.
HERB KELLEHER

Herb Kelleher founded Southwest Airlines to build a company based in love and enjoyment. His simple leadership philosophy was to have fun and make money at the same time. He questioned and disrupted the business model of the airline industry. Kelleher defined Southwest as an endeavor to give ordinary people the freedom to fly. He believed in hiring people based on their attitude, then training them in the skills required. He encouraged his people to observe, listen to, and understand each other's stresses. Through his Walk a Mile program, employees traded jobs. He actively listened to all he met, leaving his own ego at the door. Kelleher promoted independent thinking, taught others to not take themselves too seriously, and challenged the status quo. His business model used scenario planning, not strategic planning, so his leaders were prepared for all possible issues and threats that could occur. Herb's teams learned to think and act with love, fun, and flâneur. His wisdom, composure, and happiness were contagious for employees and customers alike.

Miguel Cabrera: Baseball Award Winner, Philanthropist, Community Servant[50]

How can I feel pressure doing what I love to do? I'm just trying to play my best and have fun.
   JOSE MIGUEL CABRERA TORRES

Jose Miguel Cabrera Torres, known worldwide as "Miggy," was the most successful Venezuelan to play American Major League Baseball. He retired with dozens of records as one of the top ten players of all time. Yet, his success is little known outside of baseball circles because he handled his career with a very quiet demeanor. He spent most of his career with the Detroit Tigers when they were a mediocre team, choosing not to chase World Series fame. He learned English early in his career but did not become a clubhouse spokesperson. Instead of drawing attention to himself via marketing, branding, and social media, he put his efforts into establishing a foundation to support young athletes and help re-build the Detroit community. His work is little known because he prefers to contribute without fanfare. He let his hitting and performance on the field be his contribution to the leadership of the team. Unlike many professional athletes, he is a philanthropist because he wants to give back, and because he enjoys it, not to gain fame or make more money. His flâneur is based in steady performance and having a behind-the-scenes impact on young people's lives.

Michelle Obama: Community Relations Executive, Author, First Lady of the United States[51]

I spent much of my childhood listening to the sound of striving.
                                   MICHELLE OBAMA

Michelle LaVaughn Robinson Obama was a high achieving woman from an early age. A Harvard Law School graduate, she was powerful and influential in several top-level administrative positions at the University of Chicago. She was one of the most accomplished women to serve as First Lady of the United States. Yet, her demeanor was always laid-back as she checked off her achievements. With grace and finesse, she calmly took the back seat to the President. In the background, she quietly coordinated complex initiatives across several government agencies. She established Joining Forces to support employment, education, and wellness for U.S. service members, veterans, and their families. Post-White House, she continues to wield her power with flâneur, carefully and wisely using social media to influence social change and solve world problems. Through her writings, Michelle influences and inspires others' personal development. She stays under the radar yet has a big impact.

Angela Merkel: World Leader, Chancellor of Germany, Social Change Agent[52]

It's always important that I go through all the possible options for a decision. I always wanted to know what I'd face next, even though that was maybe a bit detrimental to spontaneity. Structuring my life and avoiding chaos was more important.

ANGELA MERKEL

As the first female chancellor of Germany, Angela Dorothea Merkel's collaborative and pragmatic style kept her in power for 16 years. She was considered tactically brilliant, and one who could maintain stability through a crisis. She logged continuous accomplishments and improvements, calmly leading the country through the 2008 financial crisis, Brexit, and an immigration crisis. Merkel understood she needed a fact-based and skilled communications approach to counteract Germans' suspicion of charismatic leaders. She addressed challenges and solved problems by listening, then encouraging dialogue and compromise. She welcomed refugees from Syria when other European Union states closed their borders. Merkel created an effective system to provide language studies and skills training, then integrate them into the work force. This strengthened the German economy. She brought the EU states together with her careful and enduring diplomacy. Angela Merkel became respected for her ability to spread optimism across the globe. Germany's economy and political system flourished because of her flâneur.

CONCLUSION

Using the Flâneur Web of Belief, we become *strollers* through life and work. As we slow down to observe and reflect on the situations we encounter, we respond appropriately to crisis and uncertainty. We develop advanced listening and questioning skills for dialogue with peers and followers. We gain competencies to solve complex problems. We practice transformational, adaptive, and servant leadership. We take time for periods of detachment and rest. We balance, and re-balance, work, life, and relationships. We learn to manage the stressors in work and life. We become calm, mindful, healthy, and wise.

ADDITIONAL RESOURCES

A Return to Love. Marianne Williamson. Harper Perennial, 1996

A Path with Heart. Jack Kornfield. Bantam, 1993

Composure: The Art of Executive Presence. Kate Purmal. Amplify Publishing, 2021

Find Your Balance Point. Brian Tracy & Christina Stein. Berrett-Kohler, 2015

How To Be Idle. Tom Hodgkinson. Harper Collins, 2005

In Praise of Slowness: Challenging the Cult of Speed. Carl Honore. Harper Collins, 2004

Practicing The Power of Now. Eckhart Tolle, Plume, 2001

Sabbath. Wayne Muller. Bantam Books, 2000

Stillness Speaks. Eckhart Tolle, Plume, 2003

The Answer is a Question. Laura Ashley-Timms & Dominic Ashley-Timms. TSO, 2022

There Is a Spiritual Solution to Every Problem. Wayne W. Dyer. Quill, 2001

The Joy of Laziness. Peter Axt & Michaella Axt-Gadermann. Hunter House, 2003

The Power of Now. Eckhart Tolle, Plume, 1997

The Precious Present. Spencer Johnson. Doubleday, 1981

CHAPTER APPENDIX

The Flâneur Web of Belief[SM]	Competencies & Mindsets Developed Within Leadership Theories and Styles
Complexity/Strategic/ Adaptive/Crisis/ Executive Leadership Capacities	Facilitator, credibility, coordinator, broker, work through conflicting constraints, resolve conflicts quickly, manage entanglement, creative tension, reflective mindset, managerial wisdom, social intelligence, engage across boundaries, focus on multiple perspectives, bring best of self to organization, transform via language, multi-level adaptive, broad behavioral repertoire, charisma[53], take responsibility for decisions, take responsibility for communications[54]
Shared/Connective/ Servant/ Team/ Leadership and Followership Capacities	Political awareness, rehearsal, vulnerability, multiple roles, work/life balance, conflict management, self-observation, emotional intelligence, inquiry, generative dialogue, self-in-relation awareness, participative goal setting, ensure different voices, patterning of attention, timing, dialogue and discussion, multiple perspectives, facilitator, cultivate undirected interactions, perspective, attribution of meaning in communications, collective perspective[50], conflict overcoming, personalize attention, engage others in conversation, be open, consider others' points of view, manage political behavior, empathy, healing, awareness, persuasion, conceptualization, ask for others' opinions, help avoid or resolve interpersonal conflicts, step back and let others decide[56], healing, awareness, persuasion, conceptualization, foresight, attention to followers, listen[57], team rehearsal, team self-talk, feedback, discussion[58], reduce stress, actively engage followers challenge leaders, reflection[59]
Authentic Leadership/ Self Leadership/ Emotional Intelligence Capacities	Positive modeling, positive psychological capital, benevolent values, heart, trust, balanced/unbiased processing, consistency, self-awareness, emotional intelligence, receiving feedback, reflective circumspection of life stories, achieve health and well-being, physical and emotional fitness, self-observation, shifting mental models, reflective mindset, social intelligence[60], physical fitness, exercise and diet, active listener, conversational skills, metacognition, self-knowledge, automaticity, meta-management of behavior, communicate at emotional level, understand others' emotions, be in tune with our own emotions, read nonverbal cues, control emotions, express feelings appropriately, social dynamic, see things from another's perspective[61]
Change Leadership & Transformational Leadership Capacities	Negotiate shared understanding, advanced interpersonal skills, personalize attention, objective inquiry, perspectivism[62], remove obstacles[63], wield power effectively, fairness, debate[64]

THE HORIZONS OF OUR LEADERSHIP

As twenty-first century leaders,
we are engaged in work greater than ourselves,
our lives, or even our organizations.

We are involved in a societal transformation
where values guide our choices for thinking and acting.

As the human and the corporate spirits evolve and change,
larger forces beckon us to pull together.

Building teams, developing talents, and engaging our people
are all part of a renewal of humanness in our world.

PAT O'CONNELL

CHAPTER 8

MAPPING YOUR LEADERSHIP & LIFE DEVELOPMENT

> For a journey anywhere, a map is a meaningful guide. To develop our leadership competencies, a unique GPS keeps us on course. Setting goals and charting plans will enrich and accelerate our growth as humans and leaders.

THE POWER OF GOAL SETTING

Every person's life depends on the process of choosing goals to pursue; if you remain passive, you are not going to thrive as a human being.
GARY LOCKE

What is a goal?
A goal is an action with an aim and a timeline. Goals empower us and control the direction of our lives. Aspiring to be good or do well are worthy intentions. But these vague intentions are impossible to track and assess. Goals provide specific and measurable outcomes[1]. The best goals define why, how, and when an action or project will be accomplished.

What makes a goal powerful?
Effective goals translate your talents, values, and passions into specific objectives. Powerful goals challenge you to do something just beyond what you believe is possible. Setting powerful goals is the most significant thing you can do to succeed in your career and your life. They contribute to self-motivation, high performance, and satisfaction in life and work. They advance your capabilities and build your confidence.

WHY YOU NEED A FORMAL PLAN

To generate energy
As leaders, we strive for competence, autonomy, and relatedness. We hope to initiate and regulate our own actions. When we work to fulfill these needs, we energize our bodies and propel our inspiration and motivation. Setting goals increases self-determination. We are driven to action and peak performance.

We commit and persist to gain advanced skillsets and mindsets. Reaching a goal is more motivational than making money[2].

To direct your efforts
A mission and vision become beacons for your leadership. Yet, these are often lofty and general. A plan with concrete tasks and specific timetables translates aspirations into expectations. Your plan becomes a blueprint and a routing guide. You are pressed into action. You improve your competencies for self-regulation and self-leadership[3].

To gain confidence
With a plan, you check your progress and realize outcomes. You gain skills and better understand the boundaries of your abilities and talents. You create a personal guide and follow through. Your confidence grows. Reaching a milestone motivates you to set even more challenging goals and put in more effort. You pursue your next plans with self-assurance and courage[4].

To be sure of your progress
Without a plan, you may know where you have been but not where you are headed. With a plan, your path is clear. You set targets and make lists of to-dos for checking and re-checking. When you fall short, you have specifics to reflect on before trying again or changing your objectives.

To increase the speed and depth of your leader development
It takes time and effort to set and map an effective plan. Yet, you save time because your goals and activities fit your dreams. Your efforts are focused and defined. You have an organized call to action. Your plan specifies items for accomplishment and timetables for progress. You easily analyze and reflect on what is complete, where more time is needed, and what needs to change. You set a direct route to achievement. Your plan motivates and accelerates your development as a leader.

HOW TO CREATE YOUR FORMAL PLAN

Do what you can with what you've got, where you are.
THEODORE ROOSEVELT

Begin with a dream
Always have a vision for five to ten years in the future. Some leaders develop plans and goals for a lifetime. They know what they want to accomplish while on this earth. Others plan from point to point in their career and life. If you wish, start with the end in mind. What would you like written on your epitaph or in your obituary? Make every goal, large or small, part of your dream. Complete the Life Dreaming exercise to uncover your life and leadership desires.

REFLECTION ACTIVITY 8-1: LIFE DREAMING

Review your values, vision, and mission before completing these charts. You might not have the answers to some of these questions. Answer what you can.

In my wildest dreams, I have always thought my life accomplishments might be or include:

If you could fast forward your life, what would you be doing or what would you accomplish?

In	I would like to be or be doing:	I would like to have accomplished or completed:
5 Years		
10 Years		
15 Years		

If money or family considerations did not matter, what would you be doing with your life right now?

What, from this reflection, will I include in my Leadership and Life Plan?

Understand the goal-setting process

Your plan must be written. Include a reflective essay explaining your purpose and expected outcomes. Break down each goal into sub-projects and concrete actions plans. Expand large projects or long-term objectives into understandable and doable tasks[5]. Timetables are imperative. By writing out your plan, you exponentially increase the probability of achieving your goals.

How and Where Should I Create My Plan?

Handwriting and sketching are the most powerful way to commit your goals to memory and to action. Research shows when we write by hand, we utilize our left and right hemispheres of our brains together. We are more creative and more committed to follow through. I recommend a journal-style planning process. Acquire a journal. Begin the journal with your initial goals and plans. Use it over time to track your progress, reflect on your actions and implementation, and revise the plan. Your journal becomes a keepsake that tells the story of your life and leadership. Write your goals and your plan in a way that fits you and fits your life.
Where and how will you record your plan?

Select a time period

Your plan may be short term, medium term, or long term. Select a timetable to fit your life and your current circumstances. Focus on your most important and relevant needs. Consider the resources and capabilities you will need to complete the plan. For example, if you are envisioning a promotion, set a short or medium term timeline for gaining the skills necessary to become deserving of the role. If you plan to buy a new home, determine a target size and location, and a financial strategy. If you are dreaming of starting your own business, identify the long term steps for the whole process. Regardless of the timeframe for the outcome, your plan must include details and specifics for the first six to twelve months.

Write the story of your plan

Your goals and your plan should tell a story. Start with a narrative explaining what you will do and why. Write a two- to three-page letter to yourself explaining the reasons you are developing a plan at this time in your life or career. Expound on your purpose, motivation, and intentions. Include a summary of your competencies and dreams. Tell how your dreams, values and mission have inspired you. Explain the leadership skills and mindsets you will need to meet your goals. Project yourself into the future to describe your results when you reach your targets.

Challenge yourself

Set difficult, but realistic, goals. Make sure they tap into your talents and interests. Be certain you are enthusiastic and really want to invest time and effort into these actions. When constructing goals, consider outcomes that are challenging yet achievable; realistic and relevant; simple and straightforward; meaningful and inspirational. Complete the energy-giving exercise for insights on what keeps you engaged in a difficult task.

SELF-ASSESSMENT 8-2: THE ENERGIES IN YOUR LIFE

List activities, people, or places which affect your energy levels.

Things that give me energy, making me motivated, inspired, more active	Things that take away my energy, making me dull, tired, unmotivated

Summarize what you learned and what you might apply to your Leadership and Life Plan:

Choose two to three milestones
As a leader who believes in purpose, set focused goals for your life and/or work. Select two or three achievable, but challenging, outcomes. They should be just beyond reach and generate excitement for you. Assign an ending date to each. Be sure your goals are things you want to commit to and engage in. If not, make changes.

REFLECTION ACTIVITY 8-3: OPTIONS FOR MY MILESTONES

Brainstorm. List ideas and options for your life and work goals.

Identify two to three leadership needs
As you plan for your goals, also think about what leadership skills or mindsets you will need to accomplish these goals. Prioritize two or three items to support the achievement of your milestones. Your goals and leadership needs are the outline for your written plan.

REFLECTION ACTIVITY 8-4: OPTIONS FOR MY MILESTONES

Brainstorm. List ideas and options for your leader development.

Do action planning
Your major goals must be translated into measurable action plans. For each milestone and leadership competency, list the actions needed to successfully achieve each goal. Use concrete language. Develop timetables. Make the action items and the timeframes challenging but doable. Remember you can edit and adjust the plan as you are working toward your goals. A sample action plan is found at the end of this chapter.

Plan for measuring
For each of your four to six major goals, write out what success will look like. How will you feel when you complete these goals? How will you know you reached the finish line? How will your life or work be changed? Make the definitions of interim steps and final objectives specific and measurable.

Plan for self-motivation
Consider adding motivational aspects to your plan. For example, select one or two inspirational songs as reminders of your dreams. Find a picture depicting your goals. Choose a podcast to learn from. Use these elements as reminders which build momentum to continue toward your destination. Be sure to include self-rewards and self-appreciation as you accomplish sub-goals and final milestones. For example, treat yourself to something. Allow yourself time to enjoy nature, family, or an activity of interest.

ACTIVITY 8-5: THE PARAMETERS OF YOUR LIFE AND LEADERSHIP PLAN

Use this chart as an idea sheet and tool to develop the outline for your Life and Leadership Plan.

Life/Work Goals	Start and End Timeframes	Talents & Skills I Will Apply	What Will Be Easy	What Will be Difficult
1.				
2.				
3.				
Leadership Needs	Start and End Timeframes	Talents & Skills I Will Apply	What Will Be Easy	What Will be Difficult
1.				
2.				
3.				

Finalize your blueprint
Using all the elements you have drafted, put your plan together into a coherent and useful format. Consider this effort as if it were a final school project and a long letter to yourself. Start with the story of your current chapter of your life and leadership story. Talk about your strengths, weaknesses, opportunities and threats. Explain your reasons and intentions. Write a creative section with the end in mind: what will life and work be or look like when you reach your

goals? For each life/career and leadership goal, provide at least two paragraphs describing the specific goal, what you aim to accomplish, and how you will approach it.

Once you have all this in writing, create charts or outlines with the major goals, detailed sub-goals, milestones, timetables for completion, and your rewards along the way. Explain or incorporate your motivational items meant to keep you aware of and motivated toward your goals. Put your document and supporting materials in a safe but accessible place. Be sure it is visible and available to guide and focus your efforts.

HOW TO IMPLEMENT YOUR FORMAL PLAN

Develop task lists
Action plans are completed over a period of weeks or months. To be sure you take regular steps toward your end goals and action plans, identify short tasks you can complete daily or weekly. Brainstorm a list of small steps and quick tasks for each action plan. Make them clear, simple, and easy to do. These are the turn-by-turn directions for your journey.

Chart and schedule
Using a planner, to-do lists, or electronic reminders, add your short tasks to daily and weekly schedules. As you write a task on your planner or to-do list, also note an estimate of the amount of time it will take. Upon completion, track the actual time for the task. This will help you schedule the time needed for similar initiatives in the future. Time-manage your plan. Make it simple and easy to navigate, step-by-step.

Be accountable
You are more likely to work your plan if you tell someone else about it. Share your goals with a friend, family member, mentor, coach, co-worker, or leader. Keep them apprised of your progress. Get support and feedback. When you hit a snag, talk it over with them for their ideas and empathy. Your supporters will help you re-engage and recommit.

Motivate yourself
Keep reminders of your dreams visible and handy. Create a vision board. Post notes about your goals on your bedroom walls, your bathroom mirror, on the way out the door, and on your devices. Find inspirational photos and quotations to keep you aware of, and committed to, your goals. Select music or songs to inspire you.

Incentivize yourself
Celebrate your progress at every turn. All the small tasks and steps do lead to big accomplishments. Remember to congratulate and reward yourself along the way. Working toward a goal can be intense and stressful. You may get

discouraged or doubt yourself. Life may get in the way. Work your plan with flâneur. Take a day, a week, or a month's breather if you need to.

Track your progress
Every month or two, review what you completed (or not) and how you managed your time. As you see how to make realistic progress toward your goals, reflect on what you did and how you did it. Write notes about what you learned. Use this feedback to adjust your efforts and your plan. Remember, no plan is perfect. You may revise or completely re-create your goals and plan at any time.

Refresh your plan and keep going
Conduct your own performance review every six months. Adjust your expectations, and know what you can get done when, where, and how. Fine-tune the action plans and/or timetables. Brainstorm about what your next plan will include. Incorporate new opportunities, newly discovered passions, and your current dreams. On a day-to-day and month-to-month basis, you will have a blueprint for purpose and meaning in your life and work. Keep dreaming and visioning. Never be without a two-year plan for your life and leadership development. Continue the micro-level action planning. Always have meaningful and purposeful to-dos on your daily calendar.

ASSESSMENT 8-6: MY PERFORMANCE AND PROGRESS REVIEW

Check your progress toward your goals every 60-90 days. Use this form to record your accomplishments.

Progress I have made on my tasks and action plans/my interim accomplishments:
Challenges I experienced along the way:
What to do/how to continue:
What to change in my plans or timetables:
Help or support I need, and how I will get it:

SAMPLE: GOALS, ACTION PLANS & TASK LISTS

GOAL: Publish My Next Book Within 24 Months

Action Plans

Month 1: Create chapter description
Month 2: Gather content already written
Month 3: Determine additional content needs
Month 4: Research: Current content
Month 5: Research: Additional content

Month 6-12: Writing Process: First draft
Month 13-17: Writing Process: refinement
Month 18-20: Writing Process: editing
Month 21-24: Publishing Process

Month 1

Task Steps

Week 1
2 hours - Brainstorm ideas for content
2 hours - Competitive analysis of similar genre offerings

Week 2
1 hour - Write purpose of book
2 hours - First draft of table of contents

Week 3
1 hour - Refine table of contents & write notes for descriptions
.5 hour - Review chapters listing & notes
2 hours - Write first draft of chapter descriptions

Week 4
1 hour - Review & edit chapter descriptions
1 hour - Second review & finalize chapter descriptions

Related Leader Development Goal: Stay Healthy & Stay Energized

Action Plans

Task 1: Improve yoga practice
Task 2: Eat heathy

Task 3: Take small breaks
Task 4: Take long breaks

Month 1

Task Steps

Week 1
10 minutes yoga every other day
3 lunch salads this week
Take 1 walk

Week 2
10 minutes yoga 2/3 days
3 lunch salads this week
Take 1 walk

Week 3
Continue yoga 2/3 days
Increase yoga to 15 minutes once this week
4 lunch salads this week
Take 1 walk
Make reservations to visit family

Week 4
Continue yoga 2/3 days
Increase yoga to 15 minutes twice this week
4 lunch salads this week
Take 1 walk

CONCLUSION

Choosing to develop as a leader is a commitment to become your best and most successful self. If you continue to use the Leader Development Webs of Belief[SM], you will experience more freedom, meaning, and satisfaction in your life and work. Continue your journey toward the mastery of learning, reverence, purpose, authenticity, and flâneur. It will require time, energy, and persistence. As you take two steps forward, you will often take one step back. Stay hopeful and determined. Simplify your thinking and planning to keep moving ahead. You will become an authentic and effective human and leader, but you will never reach perfection. You will progress in skills and wisdom for as long as you live.

Always remember our definition of leadership: to *influence yourself and others to adopt collaborative behaviors and mindsets to address mutual problems, contribute to positive outcomes, and make meaningful connections.* I believe you will use the webs of belief to develop a solid set of leadership competencies. I am counting on you to help build a peaceful world and improve the quality of life for everyone in it. I leave you with hope and expectation for the luck of the Irish.

> May the road rise up to meet you,
> May the wind be always at your back,
> May the sun shine warm upon your face,
> The rains fall soft upon your fields
>
> May everything go right, and nothing wrong.
> May those you love bring love back to you,
> and may all the wishes you wish come true.

Thank you for using this book. Please share your feedback and comments with me!

Dr. Pat O'Connell
drpatoconnell.com

Notes

Chapter 1
1. https://www.amazon.com/s?k=leadership&i=stripbooks&crid=1P7TFAWAIEBRS&sprefix=leadership%2Cstripbooks%2C94&ref=nb_sb_noss_1
   https://www.google.com/webhp?hl=en&sa=X&ved=0ahUKEwi9z8uG8sSGAxX6k4kEHXZyDawQPAgJ
2. https://www.naceweb.org/career-readiness/competencies/career-readiness-competencies-employer-survey-results
   Peter Northoose, *Leadership: Theory and Practice*. Thousand Oaks: Sage, 2015.
3. Patricia K. O'Connell, "A Simplified Framework for 21st Century Leader Development." Leadership Quarterly 25 (2014), 183-203
4. Robert Kegan, *In Over Our Heads. The Mental Demands of Modern Life*. Cambridge, MA: Harvard University Press, 1994
5. Joseph Sifakis, in *Understanding and Changing the World: From Information to Knowledge and Intelligence*, Singapore: Springer, 2022
6. https://baynews9.com/fl/tampa/news/2024/03/18/manatee-county--gun-sales---safety-classes-increase-after-desantis-signs-hb-543
   https://www.toledoblade.com/opinion/editorials/2019/10/04/florida-court-lights-the-way-ohio-mike-dewine-red-flag-law/stories/20190926185

Chapter 2
1. O'Connell, "A Simplified Framework..."
2. Stephen P. Turner, "Webs of Belief or Practices: The Problem of Understanding." *European Journal of Sociology 51* (2010): 403-427. http://dx.doi.org/10.1017/S0003975610000196.
3. Alan Dearing, "How Have 21st Century Leader Development Methods Evolved, In Relation to a Webs of Belief Framework" (master's thesis, Lourdes University, 2015)
   Candace Kwapich, "Studying the Webs of Belief as a Leadership Development Foundation and Framework" (master's thesis, Lourdes University, 2019
4. David. V. Day, Michelle M. Harrison, and Stanley M. Halpin, *An Integrative Approach to Leader Development; Connecting Adult Development, Identity, And Expertise.* (New York:Routledge, 2009)
5. Ursula Goodenough and Paul Woodruff, "Mindful Virtue, Mindful Reverence," *Zygon*, 36 no.4 (2001), 585–595.
6. Fred Luthans, and Bruce Avolio, "Authentic Leadership: A Positive Developmental Approach," in *Positive Organizational Scholarship*, ed. K. S. Cameron, J. E. Dutton and R. E. Quinn (San Francisco: Barrett-Koehler, 2003) 241–261.
7. Simmel, *The Metropolis and Mental Life*, 1903.
8. Wayne Muller, Sabbath: *Finding Rest, Renewal, and Delight in our Busy Lives.* (New York, NY: Bantam, 1999)

Chapter 3
1. Jean Piaget, *Le Structuralisme*, Paris: Presses Universitaires de France, 1968.
2. Robert Kegan, *The Evolving Self: Problem and Process in Human Development*, Cambridge, MA: Harvard University Press, 1982.

3. In John A. Barnes, *John F. Kennedy on Leadership: The Lessons and Legacy of a President*, New York: AMACOM, 2005.
4. Peter M. Senge *The Fifth Discipline: The Art And Practice Of The Learning Organization*, New York: Doubleday, 1990.
5. Robert J. Sternberg, *Wisdom, Intelligence, And Creativity, Synthesized*, New York: Cambridge University Press, 2003a.
6. https://elearningindustry.com/information-processing-basics-how-brain-processes-information
7. Krathwohl, David R. 2002. "A Revision of Bloom's Taxonomy: An Overview." *Theory Into Practice* 41 (4): 212–18. doi:10.1207/s15430421tip4104_2.
8. Eugene Mathes, "An Evolutionary Perspective on Kohlberg's Theory Of Moral Development," *Current Psychology* 40 (2021) 3908–3921 (2021). https://doi.org/10.1007/s12144-019-00348-0
9. Susan Whitbourne, Michael Zuschlag, Lisa B. Elliot, and Alan S. Waterman, (1992). "Psychosocial Development in Adulthood: A 22-Year Sequential Study," *Journal of Personality and Social Psychology* 63 no. 2 (1992), 260–271. https://doi.org/10.1037/0022-3514.63.2.260
10. Kegan, *The Evolving Self.*
11. Stephen R. Covey, *The 7 Habits of Highly Effective People, 30th Anniversary Edition*, New York: Simon & Schuster, 2020.
12. Daniel Levinson, "A Conception of Adult Development," *American Psychologist* 41 no.1, (1986): 3-13.
13. https://www.buildyoursafespace.com/post/3-types-of-life-transitions
14. Nichole Longeway, "Developing Young Minds into Tomorrow's Leaders" (master's thesis, Lourdes University, 2021).
15. Albert Bandura, *Self-Efficacy: The Exercise of Control*, NewYork: W.H. Freeman, 1997.
16. Day, Harrison, and Halpin, *An Integrated Approach...*
17. Warren G. Bennis and Robert J. Thomas, "The Crucibles of Leadership," *The Harvard Business Review,* September 2002, 39-45
18. Mary Uhl-Bien, Russ Marion, and Bill McKelvey, (2007). "Complexity Leadership Theory: Shifting Leadership from The Industrial Age to The Knowledge Age. *The Leadership Quarterly*, 18 (2007) 298–318.
19. Rosabeth Moss Kanter, *The Change Masters*, New York: Simon & Schuster, 1983
20. Charles Manz, Christopher P. Neck, and Jeffrey D. Houghton, Self-Leadership: *The Definitive Guide to Personal Excellence*, Thousand Oaks, CA: Sage, 2020.
21. Jean Lipman-Blumen, "*Connective Leadership: Managing in a Changing World*," Oxford: Oxford University Press, 1996
22. https://www.rasmussen.edu/degrees/education/blog/types-of-learning-styles/
23. Carol S. Dweck, Mindset: *The New Psychology of Success*, New York: Ballantine, 2016
24. Senge, *The Fifth Discipline*
25. Katherine and Richard Greene, *The Man Behind the Magic: The Story of Walt Disney*, New York, Penguin Books, 1991.
   Dave Smith, *The Quotable Walt Disney*, Disney Editions, New York, 2001.
26. Wooden, John R, and Steve Jamison. *Wooden*. Contemporary Books, 1997.
   John Wooden and Jay Carty, *Coach Wooden's Pyramid of Success*, Revell Press, Grand Rapids, MI, 2005
   https://www.thewoodeneffect.com/pyramid-of-success/
27. https://apple.com>podcasts>harvardstaylorswiftcourse
   https://www.britannica.com/biography/Taylor-Swift

https://press.farm/taylor-swifts-business-team-behind-her-success/#:~:text=Enter%20Tree%20Paine%2C%20Swift's%20 longtime,%2C%20merchandise%20lines%2C%20and%20partnerships/

28. https://www.britannica.com/money/Richard-Branson
Connley, C. (2017). Richard Branson says the key to success isn't a university degree. CNBC.
[cnbc.com/2017/11/29/Richard-branson-says-the-key-to-success-isnt-a- university-degree.html/
Schwabel, D. (2014). Richard branson's three most important leadership principles. *Forbes*.
https://www.forbes.com/sites/danschawbel/2014/09/23/richard-branson-his-3-most-important-leadership-principles/?sh=64f58b423d50&fbclid=IwAR3KjIyZRzRz67Zw7844ngoSBxtmcfEhX7gztGoGD9NO58lKEU9hjGgsyvs
29. O'Connell, "A Simplified Framework...
30. Ronald Heifetz, Alexander Grashow, and Marty Linsky. *The Practice of Adaptive Leadership*. (2009), Boston, MA: Harvard Business Press
31. O'Connell, "A Simplified Framework...
32. O'Connell, "A Simplified Framework...
33. O'Connell, "A Simplified Framework...
34. Kanter, *The Change Masters*
35. Bernard M. Bass, and Bruce J. Avolio, B. J. (Eds.), *Improving Organizational Effectiveness Through Transformational Leadership*, Thousand Oaks: Sage,1994.
36. Peter F. Drucker, The Effective Executive: *The Definitive Guide to Getting Things Done*, New York: Collins, 2006

Chapter 4

1. Joanne B. Ciulla, Terry L. Price and Susan E. Murphy, eds. *The Quest for Moral Leaders: Essays on Leadership Ethics*, New York: Edward Elgar, 2005
2. O'Connell, Walking in . . .
3. Goodenough and Woodruff, "Mindful Virtue"
4. Paul Woodruff and Betty S. Flowers, *Reverence: Renewing a Forgotten Virtue*, Oxford: Oxford University Press, 2014.
5. O'Connell, "A Simplified Framework...
6. Goodenough & Woodruff, *Mindful Virtue*.
7. Marianne Williamson, *A Return to Love: Reflections on the Principles of a Course in Miracles*, New York: Harper Collins, 1993
8. Woodruff and Flowers, *Reverence*.
9. Gordon Wang and Rick D. Hackett, "Virtues-Centered Moral Identity: An Identity-Based Explanation of the Functioning of Virtuous Leadership," *Leadership & Organization Development Journal*, September, 2022.
10. O'Connell, "A Simplified Framework...
11. O'Connell, "A Simplified Framework...
12. Jensen Jeffre, *Adolescence and Emerging Adulthood: A Cultural Approach, 6e*. Pearson: Upper Saddle River, NJ, 2018.
13. Nicholas Faulkner, and Diane Bailey, *The History of Tattoos and Body Modification*. Rosen Young Adult. (2018),
Vassar College WordPress "Tattoos Across Cultures," September 19, 2018. https://pages.vassar.edu 2018/09/19 indeed.com

14. Goodenough and Woodruff, "Mindful Virtue"
15. Daniel Goleman, *Social Intelligence*, Random house, 2007.
16. Bass, and Avolio, *Improving Organizational Effectiveness*. . .
17. Russ Marion and Mary Uhl-Bien, "Leadership in Complex Organizations," *The Leadership Quarterly* 12, (2001) 389–418.
18. Emily M. Hunter, Mitchell J. Neubert, Sara Jansen Perry, L.A. Witt, Lisa M. Penney, and Weinberger, E. (2013). "Servant Leaders Inspire Servant Followers: Antecedent and Outcomes for Employees and the Organization," *The Leadership Quarterly*, 24 no.2 (April 2013) 316-331
19. Loughlan Sofield, Carroll Juliano, and Gregory Aymond, *Facing Forgiveness*, South Bend, IN: Ave Maria Press, 2007.
    Kristin E. Robertson, *A Forgiveness Journal: Letting Go of the Past*. Colleyville, TX: Brio Leadership Press, 2009.
20. Roger Fisher, William Ury, and Bruce Patton. *Getting to Yes, Negotiating Agreement Without Giving In*. (3rd ed.), New York: Penguin Books
21. Greg Mortenson, *Three Cups of Tea: One Man's Journey to Change the World*, Puffin Books, 2009.
22. A.G. Rud and Jim Garrison, "Reverence and Listening in Teaching and Leading," *Teachers College Record* 112, 2010
23. James M. Kouzes and Barry Z. Posner, *The Leadership Challenge* (5th ed.). San Francisco, CA: Jossey Bass, 2012
24. Susan A. Wheelan, Creating Effective Teams: *A Guide for Members and Leaders* (5th Ed.), Los Angeles: Sage, 2016.
25. https://www.forbes.com/sites/celinnedacosta/2021/12/30/the-oprah-effectinfluential-women-of-diversity-to-watch-in-2021/
    Goudreau, J. (2021, December 10). Selling in a 'plus one' world. Forbes Retrieved March 20, 2022, from https://www.forbes.com/sites/ bridgetbrennan/2016/10/26/selling-in-a-plus-oneworld/
    https://help.pillar.hr/en/articles/6480301-tips-from-5-of-the-world-s-best-interviewers#
26. https://www.humanrights.com/voices-for-human-rights/muhammad-yunus html#:~:text=Economist%20and%20Nobel%20Laureate%20 Muhammad,helped%20 millions%20to%20escape%20poverty.
    Encyclopædia Britannica, inc. (2023, October 27). Muhammad Yunus. Encyclopædia Britannica. https://www.britannica.com/biography/Muhammad-Yunus
27. Biography. (2020 February 24). *Mother Teresa Biography*. A&E Television Networks. Mother Teresa - Quotes, Death & Saint - Biography
    Devasahayam, MG. (2016 September 5). *Mother Teresa a True Servant- Leader: The Statesman Columnist*. SPH Digital News. Mother Teresa a true servant-leader: The Statesman columnist, South Asia News & Top Stories - TheStraits Times
    https://missionariesofcharity.org
28. A&E Networks Television. (2020, September 11). Shonda Rhimes. Biography.com. Retrieved October 31, 2021, from https://www.biography.com/media-figure/shonda rhimes. Encyclopædia Britannica, Inc. (n.d.). Shonda Rhimes. Encyclopædia Britannica. Retrieved October 31, 2021, from https://www.britannica.com/biography/Shonda-Rhimes. Massabrook, N., Avila, D., & Chiu, M. (2017, February 27). Shonda rhimes-normalizing diversity - professional woman's magazine: The Working Woman's Magazine. Professional Woman's Magazine | The Working Woman's Magazine. Retrieved October 31, 2021, from https://professionalwomanmag.com/2017/02/shonda-rhimes-normalizing-diversity/
29. O'Connell, "A Simplified Framework. . .

30. Ben Ramalingam, David Nabarro, Arkebe Oqubay, Dame Ruth Carnall and Leni Wild (September 11, 2020). "5 Principles to Guide Adaptive Leadership," *Harvard Business Review.*
31. Randall Ziemkiewicz, "The Pulse Model for crisis and complexity leadership, (masters' thesis, Lourdes University, 2019).
32. Drucker, *The Effective Executive*
33. O'Connell, "A Simplified Framework...
34. Kouzes and Posner, *The Leadership Challenge*
35. Ronald E. Riggio, Ira Chaleff, and Jeanne Lipman-Blumen, The Art of Followership: *How Great Followers Create Great Leaders and Organizations*, San Francisco, CA: Wiley, 2008
36. Wheelan, *Creating Effective Teams...*
37. O'Connell, "A Simplified Framework...
38. William George, "Authentic Leadership Development," in *The Handbook for Teaching Leadership*, Thousand Oaks: Sage, 2011
39. Manz and Neck, *Self-Leadership*
40. Kanter, *The Change Masters*
41. John Kotter, *Leading Change*, Boston: Harvard Business Review Press, 2012
42. Bass & Avolio, *Improving Organizational...*

Chapter 5
1. G. F. Schueler, *Reasons and Purposes: Human Rationality and The Teleological Explanation of Action*, Oxford, England: Oxford University Press, 2003.
2. William Damon and Heather Malin, "The Development of Purpose: An International Perspective," In: *The Oxford Handbook of Moral Development: An Interdisciplinary Perspective*, Oxford: Oxford University Press, 2020.
3. Alessio Gori, Eleonora Topino, Andrea Svicher, and Annamaria Di Fabio, Towards Meaning in Life: A Path Analysis Exploring the Mediation of Career Adaptability in the Associations of Self-Esteem with Presence of Meaning," *J. Environ. Res. Public Health* 19, 2022. https://doi.org/10.3390/ijerph191911901
4. Abraham Maslow, (1968). *Motivation and Personality (3rd ed.)*, New York, NY: Harper, 1968
5. Craig E. Johnson, *Meeting the Ethical Challenges of Leadership: Casting Light or Shadow*. Los Angeles: Sage, 2015.
6. O'Connell, "A Simplified Framework...
7. David Viscott, *Finding Your Strength in Difficult Times: A Book of Meditations.* Chicago, IL: Contemporary Books, 1993
8. Victor E. Frankl, *Man's Search for Meaning*, New York: Washington Square Press, 1984
9. Paul T. P. Wong, "Victor Frankls Meaning-Seeking Model and Positive Psychology" in Ed. Alexander Batthyany and Pninit Russo-Netzer, *Meaning in Positive and Existential Psychology*, 149–184, New York: Springer, 2021,
10. Simon Sinek, *Start with Why: How Great Leaders Inspire Everyone to Take Action,* Toronto: Portfolio, 2009.
11. Edward Locke, and Gary Latham, "The Development of Goal Setting Theory: A Half Century Retrospective." *Journal of Motivation Science* 5 no. 2 (2019), 93–105 http://dx.doi.org/10.1037/mot0000127
12. https://www.americansurveycenter.org/americans-are-more-optimistic-than-you-think/#:~:text=The%20national%20picture%20shows%20a,not%20produce%2clear%20group%20differences.
13. Thomas Bailey, Winnie Eng, and Michael Frisch, Michael, "Hope and Optimism as

Related to Life Satisfaction." *Journal of Positive Psychology* 2 no. 3, (2007) 168-175
14. Manz and Neck, *Self-Leadership*
15. William George, *Authentic Leadership: Rediscovering the Secrets To Creating Lasting Value*. San Francisco, CA: Jossey-Bass, 2003
16. Kanter, *The Change Masters*
17. Marion and Uhl-Bien, "Leadership in Complex Organizations
18. Drucker, *The Effective Executive*
19. Hunter, and Neubert, "Servant Leaders Inspire. . .
20. Kouzes and Posner, *The Leadership Challenge*
21. https://www.reviewofreligions.org/38240/world-faiths-the-purpose-of-life/
22. O'Connell, "Walking the Footsteps. . .
23. Mary McMahon, "Work and Why We Do It: A Systems Theory Framework Perspective, "*Career Planning & Adult Development Journal*, 33 no. 2 (2017) 9-15.
24. Anthony K. Tjan, "Learning Optimism with the 24x3 Rule," *Harvard Business Review*, Boston: Harvard Business Publishing, 2011.
25. Martin Seligman, *Flourish*. New York: NY: Free Press, 2011
26. Edward L. Deci and Richard M. Ryan, "Self-Determination Theory and the Facilitation of Intrinsic Motivation, Social Development and Well-Being," *American Psychologist* 55 no. 1 (2000) 68-78
27. Mihalyi Csikszentmihalyi, *Optimal Experience: Psychological Studies of Flow in Consciousness*. Oxford: Cambridge University Press, 1992
28. Corey Yeager, *How Am I Doing? 40 Conversations*
29. Wayne W. Dyer, *The Power of Intention: Learning to Co-Create Your World Your Way*, 2005
30. Rita Mota and Ramon Llull, "A Theory of Organizational Purpose," *Academy of Management Review* 48 no. 2 (2023) 203–219. https://doi.org/10.5465/amr.2019.0307
31. Ramon van Ingen, Melanie De Ruiter, Pascale Peters, Bas Kodden, and Henry Robben, "Engaging Through Purpose: The Mediating Role of Person-Organizational Purpose Fit in the Relationship Between Perceived Organizational Purpose an Work Engagement," Management Revue 32 no. 2 (2021) 85-105. 21p. DOI: 10.5771/0935-9915-2021-2-85.
32. John Baldoni, *Lead With Purpose: Giving Your Organization A Reason to Believe in Itself*, New York: AMACOM, 2012.
33. Mota and Llull, "A Theory of Organizational. . .
34. https://www.brainyquote.com/quotes/ellen_johnson_sirleaf_485523
Nobel Prize Outreach AB. (2023). *Ellen Johnson Sirleaf - Biographical*. NobelPrize.org. https://www.nobelprize.org/prizes/peace/2011/johnson_sirleaf/facts/ Encyclopedia Britannica, inc. (2023, October 25). *Ellen Johnson Sirleaf*. Encyclopedia Britannica. https://www.britannica.com/biography/Ellen-Johnson-Sirleaf
https://www.google.com/search?client=safari&rls=en&q=liberia+today+2024&ie =UTF-8&oe=UTF-8 https://freedomhouse.org/country/liberia
Fray. (2023, April 17). *Ellen Johnson Sirleaf: The trailblazing leadership of Africa's first female president*. TheWoment. https://thewoment.org/ellen-johnson-sirleaf-the-trailblazing-leadership-of-africas-first-female-president/
Sucher, S. J. (2018, May 17). *Ellen Johnson Sirleaf: Moral Leadership in Action*
35. *https://www.britannica.com/money/Jeff-BezosAbout blue*. Blue Origin. (n.d.). Retrieved October 31, 2021
https://www.theguardian.com/technology/2021/feb/03/jeff-bezos-and-the-world-amazon-made https://www.aboutamazon.com/news/operations/update-on-our-vision-to-be-earths-best-employer-and-earths-safest-place-to-work
https://www.nytimes.com/2019/05/09/science/jeff-bezos-moon.html

Jeff Bezos' leadership style: *5 powerful principles to apply*. Lighthouse. (2023, October 23). https://getlighthouse.com/blog/jeff-bezos-leadership-style/

36. *I Am Malala: The Girl Who Stood Up for Education and Was Shot by the Taliban* (2013) https://www.britannica.com/biography/Malala-Yousafzai
37. https://www.google.com/search?client=safari&rls=en&q=Howard+Schultz&ie=UTF-8&oe=UTF-8 https://stories.starbucks.com/leadership/howard-schultz/
38. Ferris, L. (2023, May 12). *Simon Sinek: Who's the man behind the personal brand?* Foundr. https://foundr.com/articles/leadership/personal-growth/simon- sinek
    Menkes, J. (2011). *Better under pressure: How great leaders bring out the best in themselves and others*. Harvard Business Review Press.
    Sinek, S. (2009, September 29). *Start with why -- how great leaders inspire action | Simon Sinek | tedxpugetsound*. YouTube https://www.youtube.com/watch?v=u4ZoJKF_VuA
    https://www.benchmarkemail.com/blog/simon-sinek-quotes-will-change-your-business/#:~:text="People%20don't%20buy%20what,buy%20why%20you%20do%20it."
39. O'Connell, "A Simplified Framework. . .
40. Ronald E. Riggio, Ira Chaleff, and Jeanne Lipman-Blumen, *The Art of Followership*. . .
41. O'Connell, "A Simplified Framework. . .
42. Kouzes and Posner, *The Leadership Challenge*
43. Wheelan, *Creating Effective Teams*. . .
44. Hunter, and Neubert, "Servant Leaders Inspire. . .
45. Larry C. Spears, *Focus on Leadership: Servant-Leadership for the 21st Century*, New York, NY: Wiley, 2010.
46. O'Connell, "A Simplified Framework. . .
47. Manz and Neck, *Self-Leadership*
48. Daniel Goleman, *Emotional Intelligence*, New York: Bantam, 1995
49. Riggio, "The Top Ten Leadership Competencies. . .
50. Kanter, *The Change Masters*
51. Kotter, *Leading Change*
52. Bass & Avolio, *Improving Organizational*. . .

Chapter 6

Ralph Waldo Emerson, *Works of Ralph Waldo Emerson*, Routledge, 1901

1. Jean-Paul Sartre, *The Age of Reason*, New York: Vintage Books, 1947
2. Susan Harter, Authenticity. In C. R. Snyder & S. J. Lopez (Eds.), *Handbook of Positive Psychology*, Oxford: Oxford University Press (2002) 382–394.
3. Frank O. Walumbwa, Bruce J. Avolio, William L. Gardner, Tara S. Wernsing and Suzanne J. Peterson, Authentic Leadership: Development and Validation Of A Theory-Based Measure, *Journal of Management* 34 no. 1 (2008) 89-126. doi: 10.1177/0149206307308913
4. Boas Shamir and Galit Eilam. G. (2005). "What's Your Story?" A Life-Stories Approach to Authentic Leadership Development," *The Leadership Quarterly* 16 (2005) 395-417. doi: 10.1016/j.leaqua.2005.03.005
5. Bruce J. Avolio, and William L. Gardner, (2005). "Authentic Leadership Development: Getting To The Root Of Positive Forms Of Leadership," *The Leadership Quarterly* 16 (2005) 315-338. doi:10.1016/j.leaqu a.2005.03001
6. O'Connell, "A Simplified Framework. . .
7. Bruce J. Avolio and Tara S. Wernsing, Practicing Authentic Leadership. In S. J. Lopez,

(Eds.), *Positive Psychology: Exploring the Best in People*, Westport, CT: Praeger Publishers/Greenwood Publishing Group, 2008
8. Kegan, *The Evolving Self.*
9. Michael H. Kernis, "Toward a Conceptualization of Optimal Self-Esteem," *Psychological Inquiry* 14 (2003) 1-26.
10. Avolio and Gardner, "Authentic Leadership Development. . ."
11. Margaret Diddams and Glenna C. Chang, "Only Human: Exploring the Nature of Weakness In Authentic Leadership," *The Leadership Quarterly* 23 (2012) 593-603. doi:10.1016/j.leaqua.2011.12.010
12. Parul Saxena, "Johari Window: An Effective Model for Improving Interpersonal Communication and Managerial Effectiveness" *SIT Journal of Management* 5 no. 2. (December 2015) 134-146
13. Bennis and Thomas, "The Crucibles of Leadership"
14. Lawrence Kohlberg and Richard Hersh, "Moral Development: A Review of the Theory" *Theory into Practice* 16 no. 2 College of Education, The Ohio State University (1997) 53-59
15. Robert Terry, *Authentic Leadership Courage in Action.* Action Wheel Publishing, 1993
16. Tony Fusco, Siobhain O'Riordan and Stephen Palmer "Authentic Leaders Are. . . Conscious, Competent, Confident, And Congruent: A Grounded Theory of Group Coaching and Authentic Leadership Development," *International Coaching Psychology Review*, 10 no. 2 (2015) 131-148.
17. https://www.ey.com/en_us/consulting/is-gen-z-the-spark-we-need-to-see-the-light-report https://sylverconsulting.com/resources/authenticity_whitepaper_jun2018.pdf
18. Stephen Soldz and George E. Vaillant, "The Big Five Personality Traits and the Life Course: A 45-Year Longitudinal Study," *Journal of Research in Personality* 33 (June 1999) 208-232
19. Robert Anderson, "LeaderFire: The Alchemy of Transformation," *The Leadership Circle*, 2014. http://www.leadership circle.com
20. George, *Authentic Leadership*
21. Denison, D. R., Hooijberg, R., & Quinn, R. E. Paradox and Performance: Toward a Behavioral Theory of Complexity," *Organization Science* 6 (1995) 524–540.
22. Heifetz, Grashow, and Linsky. *The Practice of Adaptive Leadership.* . .
23. Emily M. Hunter, Mitchell J. Neubert, Sara Jansen Perry, L. A. Witt, Lisa M. Penney, and Evan Weinberger, "Servant Leaders Inspire Servant Followers: Antecedent and Outcomes For Employees and the Organization," *The Leadership Quarterly*, 24 no. 2 (2013) 316-331.
24. Daniel Goleman, *Emotional Intelligence* O'Connell, "A Simplified Framework. . ."
25. Corey Yeager, *How Am I Doing? 40 Conversations to Have with Yourself*, China: Harper Celebrate; Harper Collins Focus, 2022
26. Yeager, *How Am I Doing*
27. Jon H. Moilanen, "The Wisdom of Tacit Knowing-in-Action and Mission," *Adult Learning*, 2015. DOI:10.1177/1045159515583258
28. Williamson, *A Return To Love*
29. Yeager, *How Am I Doing*
30. Sean T. Hannah, Frank O. Walumbwa and Louis W. Fry, L. W. (2011). Leadership In Action Teams: Team Leader and Members' Authenticity, Authenticity Strength, and Team Outcomes. *Personnel Psychology* 64 (2011) 771-802.
31. Susan Michie and Janaki Gooty, Values, Emotions, And Authenticity: Will the Real Leader Please Stand Up? *The Leadership Quarterly* 16 no. 3 (2005) 441–457.
32. Lada Agote, Nakane Aramburu and Rune Lines, Authentic Leadership Perception, Trust

in the Leader, and Follower's Emotions in Organizational Change Processes, *The Journal of Applied Behavioral Science* 52 no. 1 (November 2015) 35-63. doi:10/1177/0021886315617531

33. Kouzes and Posner, The Leadership Challenge
34. James Cooper, "An Introduction to the Webs of Belief," (masters' thesis, Lourdes University, 2016).
35. Dan-Shang Wang and Hsieh Chia-Chun (2013). The Effect of Authentic Leadership on Employee Trust and Employee Engagement. *Social Behavior and Personality* 41 no. 4 (May 2013) 613-624.
36. W. Isaacson: Leadership Lessons of Steve Jobs Harvard Business Review April, 2012
Speak Your Mind Unapologetically: Apple Podcast
Nath, T. I. (2022, February 5). *How Steve Jobs changed the world.* Investopedia. Retrieved March 20, 2022, from https://www.investopedia.com/articles/personal-finance/012815/how-steve-jobs-changed-world.asp#:~:text=While%20best%20known%20as%20the,affect%20industries%20and%20lifestyles%20worldwide.
37. Encyclopædia Britannica, inc. (2023, October 20). *Jackie Robinson.* Encyclopædia Britannica. https://www.britannica.com/biography/Jackie-Robinson
Jackie Robinson and the "double V" campaign. National Museum of African American History and Culture. (2022, May 10).
https://nmaahc.si.edu/explore/stories/jackie-robinson-and-double-v campaign#:~:text=Five%20years%20before%20his%20Major,Pearl%20Harbor%20in%2 Honolulu%2C%20Hawaii
https://www.google.com/search?client=safari&rls=en&q=jackie+robinson+at+UC LA&ie=UTF-8&oe=UTF-8
38. https://gazette.com/life/dolly-parton-has-made-us-feel-loved-and-appreciated-for-decades-the-singer-songwriter-is/article_e2dc5dd0-ede8-11ee-ae01-4b6509f0adbd.html#:~:text=Dolly%20Parton%20is%20loved%20around,and%20all%20she%20 does%20philanthropically.
https://www.inc.com/robin-landa/how-dolly-parton-provides-a-blueprint-for-humble-leadership.html
https://davidjdeal.medium.com/why-authenticity-is-dolly-partons-superpower-3dd2da7c2a7d
Dolly Parton Biography: Nashville Tennessee. (n.d.). Retrieved November 01, 2021, from https://countrymusichalloffame.org/artist/dolly-parton/
https://www.southernliving.com/culture/dolly-parton-quotes#:~:text=Inspirational%20 Dolly%20Parton%20Quotes&text=%22The%20 way%20I%20see%20it,%2C%20 give%20'em%20yours.%22
39. https://www.nydailynews.com/2023/02/19/life-and-career-of-sidney-poitier/#
https://www.toledoblade.com/news/deaths/2022/01/07/oscar-winner-and-groundbreaking-star-sidney-poitier-dies/stories/20220107099
https://www.toledoblade.com/opinion/editorials/2022/01/09/editorial-dignity-defined-farewell-sidney-poitier/stories/20220109055
40. O'Connell, "A Simplified Framework. . .
41. The International City/County Management, 2021 Pandemic study
42. Drucker, *The Effective Executive*
43. O'Connell, "A Simplified Framework. . .
44. Wheelan, *Creating Effective Teams*
45. Ronald E. Riggio, Ira Chaleff, and Jeanne Lipman-Blumen, *The Art of Followership.* . .
46. Jean Lipman-Blumen, "*Connective Leadership: Managing in a Changing World,*" Oxford: Oxford University Press, 1996

47. Kouzes and Posner, *The Leadership Challenge*
48. O'Connell, "A Simplified Framework. . .
49. Riggio, "The Top Ten Leadership Competencies. . .
50. Manz and Neck, *Self-Leadership*
51. O'Connell, "A Simplified Framework. . .
52. Kanter, *The Change Masters*
53. Kouzes and Posner, *The Leadership Challenge*
54. Bass & Avolio, *Improving Organizational. . .*

Chapter 7

1. Georg Simmel, *The Metropolis and Mental Life*, In Gary Bridge, & Sophie Watson (Eds.), The Blackwell city reader. Oxford and Malden, MA: Wiley-Blackwell, 1903
2. *Un Voyageur:* https://mlgroves.com/baudelaire-a-portrait-of-a-flaneur/
3. O'Connell, "A Simplified Framework. . .
4. John Dewey, *How We Think: A Restatement of the Relation of Reflective Thinking to the Educative Process*, googlebooks.com, 2022
5. O'Connell, "A Simplified Framework. . .
6. Wendelin Kupers and Matt Statler, "Practically Wise Leadership: Toward an Integral Understanding," *Culture and Organization*, 14 no.4 (2008) 379-400.
7. Anthony W. Marker, "The Development of Practical Wisdom: Its Critical Role in Sustainable Performance," *Performance Improvement* 52 no.4 (2013) 11-21. doi:10.1002/pfi.21343.
8. https://wayne.edu/learning-communities/pdf/becoming-active-listener-13.pdf
9. Ghaye, Tony. 2010. "In What Ways Can Reflective Practices Enhance Human Flourishing?" *Reflective Practice* 11 (1): 1–7. doi:10.1080/14623940903525132.
10. Donald A. Schon, (1983) *The Reflective Practitioner*. New York: Basic Books, 1983.
11. David Boud, Rosemary Keogh, and David Walker, Promoting Reflection In Learning: A Model. In D. Boud, R. Keogh and D. Walker (eds.) *Reflection: Turning Experience into Learning*. London: Kogan Page, 1985
12. Moilanen, "The Wisdom of. . .
13. David L. Cooperrider and Diana Whitney, Appreciative Inquiry: *A Positive Revolution in Change*, Oakland, CA: Berrett Koehler, 2005
14. https://www.interaction-design.org/literature/topics/wicked-problems#:~:text=A%20wicked%20problem%20is%20a%20social%20or%20cultural%20problem%2that's,attempts%20to%20find%20a%20solution.
https://medium.com/the-liberators/articulating-paradoxical-challenges-with-wicked-questions-51378f6f66d5
15. Richard Paul and Linda Elder, *Critical Thinking: Tools for Taking Charge of your Learning and Your Life*, Boston, MA: Pearson, 2012
16. Rudolph E. Tanzi and Deepak Chopra, Super Brain: Unleashing the Explosive Power of Your Mind to Maximize Health, Happiness, and Spiritual Well-Being, New York: Harmony, 2012.
17. Donna L. Haeger and Tony Lingham, "A Trend Toward Work–Life Fusion: A Multi-Generational Shift In Technology Use At Work," *Technological Forecasting and Social Change*, 89 (November 2014) 316-325.
18. Csiksentmihalyi, *Optimal Experience*
19. Robert J. Sternberg. 2003. "WICS: A Model of Leadership in Organizations,"*Academy of Management Learning and Education*, 2 no. 4 (2003) 386–401.

20. Dilip V. Jeste, Ellen E. Lee, Charles Cassidy, Rachel Caspari, Pascal Gagneux, Danielle Glorioso, Bruce L. Miller, Katerina Semendeferi, Candace Vogler, Howard Nusbaum, and Dan Blazer, The New Science of Practical Wisdom. *Perspect Biol Med.* 62(2019) 216-236. doi: 10.1353/pbm.2019.0011.
21. Manz and Neck, *Self-Leadership*
22. Bernard Bass, B. *Transformational Leadership and Organizational Culture.* Sunny-Binghamton, 1993.
23. Heifetz, Grashow, and Linsky. *The Practice of Adaptive Leadership...*
24. Sternberg, "WICS: A Model...
25. Larry C. Spears, *Focus on Leadership: Servant-Leadership for the 21st Century*, New York, NY: Wiley, 2010.
26. Hunter, and Neubert, "Servant Leaders Inspire...
27. O'Connell, "Walking with Francis....
28. https://www.verywellmind.com/what-is-active-listening-3024343
29. Laura Ashley-Timms and Dominic Ashley-Timms, *The Answer Is a Question.* Norwich, UK: TSO/Williams Lee, 2022
30. David L. Cooperrider and Diana Whitney, *Appreciative Inquiry: A Positive Revolution in Change*, Oakland, CA: Berrett Koehler, 2005
31. Paul, *Critical Thinking*
32. Boud, *Reflection*
33. Cooperrider, *Appreciative Inquiry*
34. Daniel J. Levitin, *The Organized Mind: Think Straight in the Age of Information Overload*, New York: Penguin Random House, 2014.
35. Wayne Muller, *Sabbath: Finding Rest, Renewal, and Delight in our Busy Lives*, New York, NY: Bantam Books, 1999
36. Amy Houston, The Importance of Flaneur in Leadership," (masters' thesis, Lourdes University, 2015).
37. Jim Loehr and Tony Schwartz: *The Power of Full Engagement: Managing Energy, Not Time*, New York: Harmony Books, 2005
38. Huffington, *Thrive*
39. Jack Kornfield, *A Path with Heart*, New York: Bantam, 1993.
40. Jonah Lehrer, *Imagine: How creativity works.* Houghton Mifflin Harcourt, 2012
41. Deepak Chopra, "Exploring the 3 Dimensions of Meditation Practice," 2012. http://www.chopra.com/articles/exploring-the-3-dimensions-of-meditation-practice#sm.000190m5tx6p7esmgxu14hr2fx9b2.
42. https://hds.harvard.edu/news/2019/08/13/mainstream-meditation-and-million-dollar-mindfulness-boom. retrieved 5/15/24; https://mindworks.org/blog/history-origins-of-meditation/
43. Adriaan Potgieser, Anouk van der Hoor and Bauke M. de Jong, "Cerebral Activations Related to Writing and Drawing with Each Hand," *Plos One*, 2015. DOI:10.1371/journal.pone.0126723
44. Houston, "The Importance of Flaneur...
45. Wheelan, *Creating Effective Teams*
46. Janell L. Blazovich, Katherine Taken Smith and Murphy Smith, (2014). "Employee-Friendly Companies and Work-Life Balance: Is There an Impact on Financial Performance and Risk Level?" *Journal of Organizational Culture, Communications and Conflict*, 18 no. 2 (2014) 1-13.
47. Loehr, The Power of Full Engagement
48. Hagan, M. (2019). Volodymyr Zelensky. Current Biography, 80(9), 91–95.

49. 20 reasons Why Herb Kelleher Was One of the Most Beloved Leaders of Our Time. Forbes Jan 4, 2019
https://southwest50.com/our-stories/when-herb-met-rollin-the-birth-of-southwest-airlines/
50. Beck, J. (2023, September 12). The one award missing from Miggy's mantle. MLB.com. https://www.mlb.com/news/miguel-cabrera-s-last-chance-to-win-roberto-clemente-award#:~:text=The%20annual%20award%20recognizes%20the,never%20won%20the%20national%20award.
Database, O.-O. S. (n.d.). Miguel Cabrera - detroit tigers. OSDB. https://www.osdbsports.com/mlb/players/miguel-cabrera/philanthropy/0fad748a-3ed8-4787-97db-845155c8e7ce
https://www.brainyquote.com/authors/miguel-cabrera-quotes
51. https://www.whitehousehistory.org/bios/michelle-obama#:~:text=After%20graduating%20from%20public%20school,Juris%20Doctor%20three%20years%20later.
https://www.whitehouse.gov/about-the-white-house/first-families/michelle-obama/
52. Schubert, M. (n.d.). Angela Merkel: German chancellor in times of crisis: DW: 17.09.2021. DW.COM. Retrieved March 21, 2022, from https://www.dw.com/en/angela-merkel-german-chancellor-in-times-of-crisis/a-59197301
Van Esch, F. (2021, September 29). The secret of angela merkel's extraordinary success: Her understanding of the distinctive features of German politics. The Loop. Retrieved March 21, 2022, from https://theloop.ecpr.eu/the-secret-of-angela-merkels-extraordinary-success-her-understanding-of-german-politics/
https://www.brainyquote.com/lists/authors/top-10-angela-merkel-quotes
53. O'Connell, "A Simplified Framework. . .
54. Drucker, The Effective Executive
55. O'Connell, "A Simplified Framework. . .
56. Riggio, "The Top Ten Leadership Competencies. . .
57. Spears, Focus on Leadership
58. Wheelan, Creating Effective Teams
59. Ronald E. Riggio, Ira Chaleff, and Jeanne Lipman-Blumen, The Art of Followership. . .
60. O'Connell, "A Simplified Framework. . .
61. Manz and Neck, Self-Leadership
62. O'Connell, "A Simplified Framework. . .
63. Kotter, Leading Change
64. Riggio, "The Top Ten Leadership Competencies. . .

Chapter 8
1. Locke, "The Development of Goal Setting. . .
2. Locke, "The Development of Goal Setting. . .
3. Carol S. Dweck, Mindset: The New Psychology of Success, New York: Ballantine, 2016
4. Locke, "The Development of Goal Setting. . .
5. https://www.projectmanager.com/training/make-action-plan
6. Potgeiser, Hoor, and de Jong, "Cerebral Activation. . .

www.ingramcontent.com/pod-product-compliance
Lightning Source LLC
Chambersburg PA
CBHW070334230426
43663CB00011B/2309